Our Splendid Eucharist

Reflections on Mass and Sacrament

Raymond Moloney SJ

VERITAS

First published 2003 by
Veritas Publications
7/8 Lower Abbey Street
Dublin 1
Ireland
Email publications@veritas.ie
Website www.veritas.ie

ISBN 1 85390 805 3

10 9 8 7 6 5 4 3 2

A catalogue record for this book is available from the British Library.

Cover design by Niamh McGarry
Printed in the Republic of Ireland by Criterion Press, Dublin

*Veritas books are printed on paper made from the wood pulp of managed
forests. For every tree felled, at least one tree is planted, thereby renewing
natural resources.*

TABLE OF CONTENTS

Part III: Living the Eucharist

FOREWORD

The purpose of this book is to gather together into one place and to put into as simple a language as possible something of the riches of our tradition on the Eucharist, while keeping an eye on some new things people are saying today. The method is a series of chapters, each of which is a reflection on one aspect of the sacrament. 'Reflection' is a key word. It suggests that the book is best taken in small doses, slowly and thoughtfully, rather than being read through continuously.

A glance at the table of contents will give an overview of the topics before us. It shows that the book is divided into three parts. The first section is preparatory and some may not find it as fruitful as the other two. It describes the various parts of the Mass, giving something of their history. This is necessary in order to set the scene for the next two sections, where the main contribution of the book is contained. The central section deals with the principal points of our tradition as to what the Eucharist is. It corresponds to a pamphlet written by the author many years ago and published by Messenger Publications, Dublin, under the title *Understanding the Mass Today*. With the permission of the original publisher, it is reproduced here in a revised form. The third section reflects on the implications of the Eucharist for the life of faith generally. Each chapter in the book concludes with a quotation from various sources, ancient and modern. Those from the Holy Father, Pope John Paul II, are taken from his recent encyclical on the Eucharist, *Ecclesia de Eucharistia*.

A few of these chapters have already featured as articles in *The Irish Messenger of the Sacred Heart* and are published here with permission, but mostly these chapters have been written expressly for this book. The book's title is a phrase from a talk given in Dublin many years ago by the well-known American poet and human rights activist, Fr Daniel Berrigan SJ, and is used here with his permission.

PART I

CELEBRATING THE EUCHARIST

1 THE HIDDEN TREASURE

Some years ago there came to light in the wall of an old house in County Down in Ireland a penal chalice in the form of a shell. A penal chalice is one used for Mass during the times of the persecution of the faith in Ireland. Sometime in the early 19th century, it had been wrapped up in an old newspaper and sealed in the wall of the house, never to be disturbed until its recent recovery.

This story is an eloquent reminder of the faith of the poor and the persecuted in an older and sadder Ireland. At that time the Mass was the one thing that really mattered. Just as the blood of Christ gave a new value to an ordinary shell thrown up by the sea, so the Mass brought meaning and even beauty into lives often left without the very necessities of living.

An Ancient Faith
In the old prayers that have come down to us from the Irish language we can rediscover something of the spirit with which the poor of those times regarded the Mass. There were, for instance, the prayers which they would recite on the way to Mass. Here is one from County Kerry:

> We walk together with Mary the Virgin and with the
> other saints who accompanied her only Son on the way
> to Calvary.[1]

As soon as the church building came into view they would say:

> Blessed is the house of God – and I myself bless God –
> where he is to be found with the twelve apostles. May the
> Son of God bless us.

At the thought of approaching Christ's presence their prayer
was:

> A thousand welcomes, King of the Sunday, Son of the
> Virgin, who rose from the dead.

A Sad Contrast
Sometimes today we hear of people who complain that the
Mass is not relevant for them. Sadder still are those who have
ceased going to Mass altogether, perhaps even priding
themselves on their 'independence'. How far this is from the
spirit of the old verse, which said in Irish:

> Do not give up the Mass for anything.
> In this world there is nothing greater.
> We offer praise and deepest thanks
> to the only Son who rose from the dead.

Central Mystery of Faith
In the new liturgy we can have difficulties with the Mass which
were not there long ago. The change to the vernacular has

1. Quotations in this chapter are taken from *Our Mass Our Life*, by
    Diarmuid Ó Laoghaire, SJ, Dublin: Irish Messenger Office Pamphlet

made us more dependent on the way Mass is celebrated. Nevertheless we must keep clearly in mind that, no matter how poorly the liturgy is carried out, the Mass remains the central mystery of faith and the table of the Bread of Life. What God sets before us in the Mass is so much more significant than how people celebrate it. The same miracle of God's love for the ordinary people of this world is there waiting for us, just as it waited on our ancestors. If we do not appreciate it as they did, the difference is ultimately in us, not in the Mass.

Understanding by Living

Indeed this is part of the point in saying that the Mass is a mystery of faith. In this little book the intention is to reflect on the Mass and to try to understand it a bit more. But understanding a mystery is not like understanding a problem in arithmetic or geometry. With religious truth the explanation can bring us only part of the way. A further appreciation of the mystery will come only by living it, not just by talking about it. Mysteries of faith are more like the parables in the Gospel. They judge us. They show us up for what we are. The meaning is revealed only to those who live them, but it is concealed from those who refuse to enter into them (Mt 13:10-15).

Most likely that is why the Mass meant so much to our forebears. It was because they lived the cross in their daily lives that they could appreciate the sacrifice of the cross in the Mass. The Mass is indeed a great wonder, a stirring truth which can sustain us throughout our lives, but it is a hidden treasure that is revealed only to God's little ones. So if you find yourself saying that the Mass for you is 'irrelevant', be careful! Do not point the finger at the Mass. In the first place point the finger at yourself!

From the Eucharist the Church draws her life. From this 'living bread' she draws her nourishment.
(John Paul II)

2   THE SETTING OF THE EUCHARIST

In this book we will approach the mystery of the Eucharist in three sections. The first section will be largely descriptive. There we will go through the liturgy of the Mass in its various steps and stages as it unfolds for the Christian community, day after day, and Sunday after Sunday. In the second section we will focus on the sacramental mystery itself, trying to throw some light on its inner meaning and on the way it has been understood by the great saints and teachers of the Church. The subject of the third section will be what we will call 'a Eucharistic way of life,' reflecting on the significance of the Eucharist for our spiritual journey and on how it can give shape and form to a whole outlook on life.

The Parts of the Mass

The liturgy of the Mass as we have it today is the fruit of the reforms begun by the Second Vatican Council. This was the great gathering of all the bishops of the Catholic Church, which met in Rome over the years 1962–1965, debating on how the Church was to meet challenges of the modern world. In their teaching on the liturgy the bishops tell us that the Mass is divided into two main parts, the liturgy of the word and the liturgy of the Eucharist. Each of these has a different origin in the life of our Lord. The liturgy of the word goes back to worship in the synagogue, in which our Lord and the apostles used to take part every sabbath (Lk 4:16). The liturgy of the Eucharist, in the strict sense of that term, has its origin, as will be explained in more detail later, in the prayer customs of the Jewish home. Sometime during the first century of the

Christian Church, these two forms of liturgy were brought together and formed into the one composite celebration which we call the Mass. In the course of time a few introductory and concluding rituals were added, so that the entire Mass can now be broken up into four main parts as follows:

a)   the Opening Rites
b)   the Liturgy of the Word
c)   the Liturgy of the Eucharist
d)   the Closing Rites.

In this, the first of the book's three main sections, we will consider each of these parts in turn and the various rituals of which they are composed.

A Rich History

As a people familiar with the prayers and rituals of the Mass, we usually experience them in a routine way, accepting them one after the other without further thought. What the following pages hope to do is to suggest something of the rich history which lies behind these rituals. Knowing something of that history gives one a sense of being part of a whole multitude of Christians over the centuries who have found their way to God through these familiar rites. We are not alone when we gather for worship, but we do so 'surrounded by so great a cloud of witnesses' (Heb 12:1). What proved a support and a comfort for so many generations in the past will surely prove a support and comfort for us, as we, in our turn, try to follow them on our way back to God.

The Setting of the Sacrament

The central ritual of the Mass, namely prayer in bread and wine, comes from our Lord himself, but the sum total of what he laid down could be carried out in less than two minutes. Clearly our Lord did not expect us to charge into our chapels on Sundays for two minutes and then to move out again. He left it to the Church, or, more precisely, to the Holy Spirit working in the Church, to develop a fitting setting for what he had laid down. In this way the liturgy of the Mass has been built up over the centuries, always under the guidance of the Holy Spirit. It is this Spirit who helps the Church to change and adapt the setting, while the inner core of the Eucharist, laid down long ago by Christ himself, remains the same.

The Simplicity of the Rite

Knowing something of how the liturgy of the Mass came about over the centuries helps us to remove a false kind of halo with which it has sometimes been surrounded. One of the most striking things about the Mass, in both of its main parts, is its simplicity and straightforwardness. Our Lord did not wish to bowl us over with the magnificence of ritual. The simplicity of his worship reflects the simplicity of his life generally. An elaborate ceremonial easily develops a life of its own, whereas the important thing for our Lord was always how his followers would practise what they preach and live out in their ordinary lives the commitments they make in the Mass.

Neither Drama nor Mime

One of the mistaken ways of understanding the Mass, which has arisen from time to time in the past, is to see it as a kind of passion-play. The actions of the priest and his ministers have sometimes been understood as a kind of mime of what our Lord did at the Last Supper and on the cross. In the case of the Eucharist in particular, this way of looking at it fails to appreciate how our circumstances are now so different from those in which the foundational events of our liturgy first occurred. For one thing, our Lord himself is no longer visible before us. For another, the customs of the times are completely different. The Eucharist is not a drama following the external course of the events it is based on; it is more like a ballet, bringing out the inner meaning of those events in a form adapted to our ways of thinking.

This does not mean, of course, that the Mass is as plain as a pike-staff! There remains a depth of mystery in our liturgy which we can never fully understand; but let us locate that mystery where it really lies. It is not just a matter of signs and symbols which puzzle us. The central mystery is the reality of divine love offering itself to all in Christ's death and resurrection, and then bringing that offer into the life of the Church and into the life of each individual. To try to throw some light on this mystery, without trying to remove it, is one of the main aims of this book.

> In the words of the sacred liturgy, the Eucharist is 'the mystery of faith'.
> (Paul VI)

3   THE OPENING RITES

The Trinity
Every Mass begins, as it ends, with the invocation of the Trinity. 'I rise up today in the power of the Trinity,' says the ancient Irish prayer, the Breastplate of St Patrick. Priest and people begin every Mass in the same spirit as they bless themselves in that name which was first invoked over them at their Baptism. The revelation of the Trinity is the centre-piece of Christian truth, so that there is a special solemnity and appropriateness in invoking the God of Christian revelation as we open and close the principal celebration of the Christian faith.

The Greeting

After blessing ourselves in the name of the Trinity, the priest greets the people, a custom that is found also in the ancient Church. We read of the practice as far back as St Augustine greeting his congregation of African Christians in the fifth century. Following on the solemn invocation of the Trinity, it is a reminder that our worship has a human meaning as well as a religious one. While the form of the greeting may vary, the Missal suggests certain phrases with which Paul greeted his people in the letters he wrote to them. The simplest of these is the familiar, 'The Lord be with you,' which will be heard a number of times in the course of the Mass, expressing the special union between priest and people. The most impressive greeting is the Trinitarian one with which Paul concluded one of the most personal of his letters, the second to the Corinthians: 'The grace of the Lord Jesus Christ, the love of God and the fellowship of the Holy Spirit be with you all' (2 Cor 13:13).

The Act of Penance and Reconciliation

In the history of the ancient Roman liturgy we read that when the Pope used to arrive at the altar, he spent a few moments in silent adoration before proceeding with the service. In time this silent prayer was interpreted as a brief recollection of sinfulness and unworthiness in approaching the altar of God. Today it has been expanded into a joint acknowledgement, by priest and people alike, of the common burden of our sinfulness and of our need for God's mercy.

In some seasons of the year this ritual can be emphasized more than at others, but given its location at the beginning of the Mass, it can scarcely at any time be considered a major exercise of penitence and conversion. However for people who have just come in off the street, it is appropriate to be reminded, however briefly, that in coming to Mass, we are not there to pay God a compliment. We are his weak and wayward people, always in need of his healing mercy – and this healing power comes to us, not simply through this brief ritual, but as an aspect running through the entire Mass.

At the same time, in the western world, where the spirit of criticism and self-righteous indignation is so much a part of our newspapers and talk-shows, there is a particular fittingness in this simple but eloquent ritual. The Catholic Church openly acknowledges that it is a Church of sinners, not one just for the elite or those already saved. By 'Church' here we mean the actual Church of Pope and bishops and Mrs Murphy our next-door neighbour. We come to Mass out of a sense that we can be saved only by being part of this actual Church. The Church is Noah's ark, that saves the people from the Flood. It is the bark of Peter, that saves the disciples from the storm. There are all kinds of people in that bark, and that is why, to enter it, you need the spirit of forgiveness.

Sometimes people give as their reason for no longer going to Mass their indignation at the shortcomings of Christians or their leaders. Strangely, whatever grounds might sometimes be given for such an attitude, that one cannot be part of an authentic Christianity. Ours is a religion, not for the perfect, but for the imperfect (cfr Mt 9:13). Indeed, Christianity is primarily about forgiveness and compassion, seeing oneself in all sinners and all sinners in oneself. No community can keep together without that spirit of forgiveness, so that when this spirit is absent in the hearts of some people, it is no wonder that they often separate themselves from the worshipping community. The reason for their absence is not really whatever is lacking in others, but the lack within themselves of the grace celebrated in this opening ritual. It is like being without the wedding-garment, and without that one cannot enter at all (Mt 22:11-13).

Lord Have Mercy – Kyrie Eleison

In our present liturgy the triple prayer, 'Lord have mercy' comes as an extension of the act of penance, but in fact this brief prayer has a very different origin and a rich history behind it. Its beginnings lie in an ancient litany, a fact that was more obvious before Vatican II, when each of the phrases was repeated three times, making a ninefold petition in all. Some have related the three successive phrases to the three persons of the Trinity, but this does not seem to be the original notion. The word 'Kyrios', 'Lord', is used here in its New Testament sense as a name for the victorious Christ raised to God's right hand. The prayer is remarkable in being an ancient prayer to Christ, even though it has been realized from early times that the dominant movement of liturgy is prayer *through* Christ to the Father.

We first hear of this petition in its Greek form, Kyrie eleison, in the liturgy of fourth-century Jerusalem, and it may well be because of the special influence of the holy city on the pilgrims who came to it that this phrase was carried back, in the original Greek, to places where the liturgy was not in Greek, such as Egypt, Syria and Rome itself. There is even a saying in the Book of Armagh, going back to the seventh century, according to which the Kyrie eleison is seen as a link between Ireland and Rome. It suggests that the prayer, in its original Greek, came to be recognized in non-Greek lands as a token of unity among Christians.

The Gloria

By way of contrast, the liturgy now moves from humble petition to joyful praise, as the congregation takes up the song of the angels over the manger, 'Glory to God in the highest and peace to his people on earth' (Lk 2:14). Originally this prayer came from the Divine Office into the Mass of Christmas Day, but soon became such a favourite that it spread to other feasts as well. It is surely one of the most striking and popular prayers in the entire liturgy. When translated into song, it has given rise to some of the greatest masterpieces of western musical genius, but, more importantly, it is the first major expression in the Mass of the liturgy's fundamental theme, namely the praise and thanksgiving from which the Eucharist draws its name.[2]

Originally the Gloria was a hymn from the morning office, but it passed into the Roman Mass as long ago as the sixth century. In those distant days the Christians liked to face eastward in their prayer, seeing the rising sun as a symbol of the coming of Christ – destined to come at the end of time to save the world definitively, but anticipating that coming every day by rising over just and unjust alike (Mt 5:45), coming also to every congregation of his people gathered for the liturgy. In this prayer the local church becomes aware of how its liturgy is enfolded in the greater liturgy of heaven, where our High Priest is seated at the right hand of the Father, making intercession on our behalf (Rom 8:34). The liturgy of heaven is the ultimate reality of which our liturgy on earth is but the manifestation. Focusing on the heavenly liturgy at this point helps to set the scene for all that follows. It brings home to us that our gathering for Mass is not just another kind of public meeting, or even just a prayer group, but that it is part of a mystery of worship in which heaven and earth are drawn into one.

The hymns of the Church are a part of the liturgy which have to be reformed every so often. In this the early Church was no different. We read of a fourth-century council in Syria excluding from public worship all non-biblical hymns. A few exceptions were made for hymns of outstanding quality, and the Gloria is one of these (the 'Te Deum' is another). Thus this

---

2. 'Eucharistia' is the Greek word for thanksgiving

ancient text brings us back to the world of early Christian prayer.

This fact helps explain a feature of this text which might surprise us at first, namely that it is not a Trinitarian prayer. The Holy Spirit is mentioned only at the very end, and that seems to be a later addition. Originally the divinity was invoked much as Paul does in the beginning of most of his epistles, where he speaks usually of only two persons of the Trinity, 'God our Father and the Lord Jesus Christ.' This way of approaching the Godhead helps emphasize the humanity of the Second Person and the role he played in his human life and continues to play as the one mediator between God and the world. As our worship is built on the mediation of Christ, so our Mass begins with Christ the mediator.

The Collect

The introductory rites of the Mass come to a conclusion with one of its most solemn prayers, the Collect. The name 'collect' comes from the ancient Church of Gaul, indicating that this prayer is meant to collect into one all the desires and petitions that the faithful bring to every Mass. This helps explain the rather general character of the prayer. Essentially it is a universal prayer, one everyone can identify with, and so it is the first of what are called the 'presidential prayers' of the Mass, namely those which the celebrant prays as representative of the entire people of God. This is why free composition is not appropriate at this point in the service. That can have its place elsewhere in the liturgy, for instance in the Bidding Prayers; but at this point the official text helps express the unity of this local congregation with the rest of the Church throughout the world.

The saints and writers of the ancient Church in Rome seem to have had a special genius for composing this kind of prayer. Their practice of rhetoric and their strong sense of the universal in human nature came together in providing us with a number of texts which survive to this day in many of our Sunday collects. Unfortunately much of their qualities of expression have been lost in translation into English, but it is something to be borne in mind that these prayers have such a long history behind them and have been prayed by generations of Christians, by our ancestors and innumerable saints down through the centuries.

One little detail, easily overlooked, helps to underline the special solemnity of the collect. Some of our presidential prayers end with the brief phrase, 'through Christ our Lord', but, at the more significant moments of the liturgy, a longer ending is required, namely one that invokes the Trinity: '... through our Lord Jesus Christ, your Son, who lives and reigns with you and the Holy Spirit, one God, for ever and ever. Amen.' It is noteworthy how the Church underlines the special significance of the collect by requiring us to conclude this prayer with the full image of the Christian God as Father, Son and Holy Spirit. But this familiar phrase, which has become a routine for most of us, in fact sums up another basic aspect of our worship. It is prayer through Christ to the Father. As St Augustine (d. 430 AD) once put it in his discourse on the 85th psalm: in one respect, Christ prays for us; in another, he is prayed to by us. He prays for us as our priest; he is prayed to by us as our God, because in praying we must not separate the Son from the Father.

The Opening Rites Concluded

With the praying of the collect, the first of the four main parts of the Mass comes to an end. The prayers of this stage are so brief and so familiar that frequently they can slip past us without any great attentiveness on our part. That does not mean, however, that they have failed in their purpose. The main aim of these opening rites is to help us to settle down and to build a bridge between our mood in coming in off the street and our openness to the word of God. These initial acts of the assembly are not to be dwelt on excessively, for instance the celebrant's opening greeting or the rite of penance, because the people are not yet ready for great exhortations. There is surely a deep wisdom in the traditional rhythm of these opening rites, as the Church leads us gradually up to the first major act of the liturgy, which is not a human word at all, but the word of God himself.

> *I rise up today in the power of the Trinity.*
> St Patrick's Breastplate

4 CELEBRATING THE WORD

One of the great scenes of the New Testament was that day when our Lord gathered the people around him in a desert place and taught them from morning to evening about the things of God. It is remarkable that, though we have several different accounts of the event, none of them tell us anything about what he actually said. We can only assume that he taught along the lines of the Sermon on the Mount, and that, as in other parts of the Gospels, he told them story after story about the kingdom of God. Then as the sun began to go down and the shadows to lengthen, the Lord's ministry reached its climax in a wonder which so overwhelmed the disciples that it eclipsed everything else in their memory of the day. Our Lord fed the multitude with a handful of loaves and fish. By this prophetic act he was not only indicating to them that the fulfilment of their desires for the kingdom would come about through him, but he was also giving them a sign of wonders yet to come, when he would feed them with the Eucharist.

The Two Tables

It is out of events such as this that Christians have come to the idea that our Lord wishes to nourish us, not at one table only, but at two. As well as the table of the sacrament, indicated in our story by the miracle of the loaves, there is also the table of the word. Not by bread alone are we to live, but by every word that proceeds from the mouth of God (Mt 4:4). Similarly in the story of the disciples on the Emmaus road, before our Lord set before the two runaways the mystery of the breaking of bread, he first set their hearts on fire, as they walked with him on the way, by breaking to them the bread of God's word. The one 'table' prepared them for the other, and so it is in the Mass.

The Mass, as we saw at the outset of this book, is the coming together of two liturgies, that of the word and that of the Eucharist. Despite the origins of these two liturgies in two different aspects of our Lord's life, they now belong together, according to that pattern of word and sign which we have from our Lord himself in the scenes we have just mentioned. In every Mass our Lord comes before our congregations as he came before the multitude on that day in the desert, and he sets before us, as he set before them, the two tables of word and sacrament.

God Present in His Word

One of the great truths of Vatican II – one which many of us have failed to appreciate even still – is the truth about our Lord's presence in his word (*Liturgy Constitution*, art. 7). We have been reared to such a reverence for our Lord's unique presence in his sacrament that we often fail to do justice to the other modes of his presence, and in particular to his presence in his word. If we are not careful, the liturgy of the word can appear as simply someone reading a book at you, but in the context of the Mass it has to be much more than that. Already in this part of the Mass there is a Eucharistic quality in so far as the reading and preaching of God's word make God himself present to us.

Usually words are for the communication of ideas; they give information. This is true in the liturgy also, but here there is more. The word of God is not just information but formation. It not only communicates an idea; it communicates something of the reality spoken about. The word of God is a word of power, an efficacious word (1 Thess 2:13). In it God himself is at work to change us, so that in listening to this word we must not only think of applying its ideas at some future date but of accepting the presence of God within his word here and now. By truly listening to what is being read, we are letting that word of power enter into us to change us by the grace of which it speaks.

This sacramental quality of the word of God reaches its climax in the Gospel. Here we evoke the presence of Christ, but Christ present in such a way that once again he reaches out to his people with the message first heard along the roads of Galilee. In the mystery of the Mass, Belfast is Bethsaida and California is Capharnaum. On the lips of his readers and priests the voice of Christ is heard again, bringing to our generation those life-giving words which have sounded down the long line of our ancestors, have formed the civilization of the western world and will continue to sound until the end of time to form and judge the history of the race.

The Book of the Church

Indeed in this context we discover something of the true meaning of the Bible. The Bible is not just another book. Books as we know them are written to be read by individuals, whether in their studies or at their firesides, and to be lined up in the shelves of their libraries. The Bible was written to be proclaimed in liturgy. It is essentially the book of the Church at prayer. Paul wrote his letters to be read before the worshipping congregations at Rome and Corinth. The Gospels were drawn up with similar audiences in mind. These writings were not written primarily for individual study but in order to form the community around the revelation of God. It is only in the Church and in the context of its prayer and authority that the Bible finds its providential place and primary meaning. Every other use of the Bible, in study or private prayer, depends on that primary experience and the meaning there found in God's word.

In considering the word of God in the liturgy, we can easily miss the wood for the trees. We get fixed on the particular passages of a particular day, and at times, it must be admitted, they can be a problem to us. But as well as looking at the individual passages, we must not lose sight of the larger picture. The basic purpose of the Bible in the liturgy is to bring before us the whole history of salvation. Each particular reading has its place only within this larger context. It is the story of God's dealings with his people, and the aim is to draw all our lesser stories into this one great story, where they are given their place and find their meaning. Through the Mass our lives become sacred lives and, like Moses and Mary and the prophets and apostles, we come to play a role in the fulfilment of God's promises.

Given that so much is offered to us in the liturgy of the word, all this must imply something about our attitude and our response. To put it briefly, it must be not just a matter of hearing but of listening. Hearing is passive, listening is active. It is not enough just to let the word of God sound in our ears. We must approach it with attention and eagerness, anxious to profit and to let it change us. First we must try to understand what we can, but in this word, because it is God's word, there are always many things which escape us. Nevertheless we must

open our hearts to these also, asking the Lord to work in us all
the graces of which he speaks, whether we understand them or
not, and so to draw our lives into the great story of his love.

> *For this reason we always give thanks to God that, on receiving
> the word you heard from us, you welcomed it, not as a word of
> human beings, but as what it is in all truth, a word of God,
> which is a power at work also among you who believe.*
> (1 Thess 2:13)

5   WORD AND SACRAMENT

One of the notable features of the restored liturgy since Vatican
II is the way the Church introduces each of its sacraments and
sacramentals with a celebration of the word of God. There is
an important principle behind this practice. All the sacraments
are sacraments of faith, as the council itself tells us (*Liturgy
Constitution*, art. 59). This means that they are not magic. Their
effect within us is conditioned by the quality of faith we bring
to them. Now Sacred Scripture is one of the main ways we have
for deepening the quality of our faith. Faith, says the council in
another place, is born of the word and nourished by the word
(*Ministry and Life of Priests*, art. 4). Consequently the celebration
of the word of God in conjunction with each sacrament helps
to dispose us to receive the sacraments at a greater depth and
with greater fruit.

The Eucharist Needs the Word

What is true of all the sacraments is true in a special way of the
Mass. Here word and sacrament belong together to form one
single act of worship. The Eucharist needs the word and the
word needs the Eucharist. The liturgy itself says of this
sacrament that it is 'the mystery of faith.' Faith therefore is
crucial for entering into the sacrament as we should, and as we

have just seen, one of the main ways of deepening faith is through the word of God.

This order of things is set before us very clearly in the two Gospel scenes in which we have already seen a blue-print of the mystery of the Mass. Before the sign of the breaking of the bread in the desert, our Lord spent the whole day in the ministry of the word. On the way to Emmaus, before he sat down at table with them, he first set his disciples on fire with his explanation of the scriptures. Unless we first experience Christ's presence in the mystery of his word, we shall scarcely recognize his presence in the breaking of the bread.

The Word Needs the Eucharist

But the reverse is also true. In itself the ministry of the word is not enough. Nowhere is this more obvious than in the story of our Lord's own life. For three years he carried out his ministry of the word the length and breadth of Galilee. His disciples were constantly with him, sitting at the feet of the greatest teacher the world has ever heard, admitted to the noblest friendship the world has ever known – but the end of it all was total failure. They took to their heels and left him to his fate, and Christ died alone.

The Christian Church never really got under way until Christ came back from the grave in the power of his death and resurrection. It is the combined power of these two events which seems to make all the difference, and it is the same in the Mass. In the Church's celebration of the word of God, Christ's ministry of the word lives again; but this is no more enough for us than it was for the first disciples. We have to move on to the mystery of his death and resurrection, made actual for us through the second half of the Mass, before we will find the strength to practise what we preach and to bring our lives into union with that of Christ.

The Whole Mystery of Christ
This reflection also gives us an impressive way of thinking of the Mass as a whole. Just as the liturgy of the word relives Christ's life, and the liturgy of the Eucharist relives his death and resurrection, so the Mass itself can be understood as a bringing together of Christ's life, death and resurrection into one ritual event before us. Through the Mass the whole mystery of Christ is made actual in the Church, so that every so often we may plunge our lives into his and in that way renew the energy and power that flow from him to us.

From this too we can also understand something of the necessity of sacraments generally in our Christian lives. For us Catholics the Church and its sacraments are crucial for the living of the Christian life. Time and again in the modern world we find people making a distinction between Christ and his Church: they accept Christ, they claim, but not his Church. Such a division is impossible. The Church is where Christ makes his grace available to us. If we separate ourselves from the Church, we separate ourselves from Christ, and without me, says our Lord, you can do nothing (Jn 15:5).

It is one thing to know what the teaching of Christ demands; it is another to put it into practice. Again and again we see that once people drift away from the Church, they begin to drift way from Christ's way of life. It might not always be obvious in the case of an individual, but on the level of society generally it soon becomes apparent. Christ's teaching makes a lot of sense of human life, but to live that life as Christ wants us to live it, is something that lies beyond our own unaided efforts. Only if we are living as members of his body, receiving through the sacraments the power of his resurrection, can we truly begin to live in his way.

Were not our hearts burning within us as he spoke to us on the way and opened up the scriptures to us?
(Lk 24:32)

6 THE LITURGY OF THE WORD

The Parts of the Liturgy of the Word
In its structure our liturgy of the word is basically the synagogue service of the Jews. We have already mentioned how our Lord usually went to the synagogue on the sabbath according to the custom of believing Jews (Lk 4:16). The apostles were in the same tradition, and continued to frequent the synagogue for some years after the Lord's resurrection. In time the split between Jews and Christians widened, and the followers of Jesus became more and more unwelcome in the synagogue. This was one reason why they began to organize their own celebrations of God's word, adding to the reading of the law and the prophets the letters and writings of the apostles. Eventually these celebrations were incorporated into the Mass, giving us the liturgy of the word as we know it.

The Jewish celebration of the word of God was composed of three main parts, the reading, the preaching and the prayers. It is easy to recognize these three aspects in our own service, which on Sundays has now been expanded into nine parts altogether:

1) Introduction to the Readings
2) Reading I
3) Psalm and Antiphon
4) Reading II
5) Acclamation (and Sequence)
6) Gospel
7) Homily

8)   Creed
9)   Bidding Prayers.

The reading of the Old Testament in the Christian service goes back to the very origins of this liturgy, since at the beginning the Old Testament was the only form of the scriptures acknowledged by Christians. Gradually the New Testament was added, and even some texts never recognized as scripture, such as the acts of the martyrs, were included. By the third century the order of the readings corresponded to the present practice of Old Testament, epistle and Gospel, though different churches followed different selections within this structure. Our present choice comes from the lectionary devised after Vatican II, and has in fact been admired and adopted in several other denominations as well.

The Gospel
The celebration of the Gospel is the high point of the liturgy of the word. This explains the special ritual with which this part of the Mass is surrounded, inspired by the idea that the reading of the Gospel brings about a real presence of Christ himself: 'The mouth of Christ is the gospel,' said St Augustine.

From ancient times the book of the Gospels has been greeted as though it were a person. In the Roman world any public representative would be greeted with lights and incense; here these marks of respect are transferred to Christ present in his word; and from ancient Gaul come the words of welcome, 'Glory to you, O Christ.'

During the other readings the people sit down, as was the custom in the synagogue, but for the Gospel we stand up, as a way of marking the special presence of the risen Christ; and then this reading is reserved to one of the ordained as the privilege of those who have dedicated their whole lives to the service of the word.

The Homily

After the Gospel a homily should normally follow, at least on Sundays and feastdays. This corresponds to the pattern our Lord himself followed in the synagogue. The purpose of the homily is to make the readings actual for our contemporaries and to build a bridge between the world of scripture and that of today. Its content should be dominated by the message of God's word rather than by the purely personal reflections of the preacher. It is still a part of God's presence through his word, for, as Paul VI put it, 'When the word of God is preached, he is present' (Encyclical *Mysterium fidei*). The homily, in the words of one writer, 'transforms the assembled community into a Church which hears the word, the Church contemplative' (H. U. von Balthasar).

> *Christ is present in his word, since it is he himself who is speaking when the holy scriptures are read in Church.*
> Vatican II

7   RESPONSE TO THE WORD

Once the word of God has been proclaimed, it is natural for the people to respond. Their response can be seen in three stages: firstly, and formally, in the recital of the creed; secondly, the Bidding Prayers are a form of response also; but there is a sense in which the whole ensuing liturgy of the Eucharist can be seen as part of the Church's response to the invitation of God revealed in his word. Our worship of God is not something that begins from below. It is something that begins with God and his revelation, and that invitation of the calling God, asking us to return to him, can be seen as the sub-text of the entire celebration of the word.

The Creed

The people's immediate response to the word read and preached is the communal reciting of the creed. The version of this prayer which we usually follow is that called the Nicene Creed. Its origins go back to the first ecumenical council of the Church, that of Nicaea in the year 325, but in fact it went through more than one edition before reaching the form in which we have it, which comes to us from another great council, that of Constantinople in the year 381. We might also note that the Nicene Creed is no dry list of doctrines, and this is why it was preferred for public worship over the creeds of other councils. It is the confession of the events through which the Word of God entered the world of time to redeem us. In this way the people mark their response to the great story of the history of salvation in the scriptures by solemnly reciting the heart of it all in the story of Jesus from eternity to eternity.

The background in the early councils helps explain the plural form in which now we recite the prayer in English: we believe. The creed is the fruit of a communal act of faith by those early councils, in which our communities now share. The plural form was commonly the custom in the Eastern Church. In the Latin Church, until recently, we followed the practice of the baptismal creeds in proclaiming our faith in the singular: I believe (Latin: *credo*), and this remains the norm in some languages.

The use of the creed in the Mass dates from the sixth century in the East. The practice eventually spread to the West through a circuitous route: Spain, Ireland, the kingdom of the Franks, reaching Rome only in the eleventh century. It seems that Irish monks had a lot to do with spreading the practice on the continent.

The purpose of the creed at this point of the Mass may be seen as twofold: looking back and looking forward. Its main purpose is to enable the people to express their response to the readings that have gone before. Just as, in a famous scene in the Old Testament, when Moses told the people about God's words and laws on the mountain, they were invited to express their consent (Exod 24:3), so in every Mass the creed gives us an opportunity of indicating our assent to God's word. The way we do that is in confessing our faith before the world (Mt 10:32). Our going to Mass at all, it must be said, is a public witness to that faith, but here, at this point of the Mass, that aspect of our worship is brought out in a solemn and public way.

But in another sense the recital of the creed looks forward to the mystery which is about to take place. There is a certain similarity between it and the Eucharistic Prayer. In one way the Eucharistic Prayer can have about it something of the quality of a creed, celebrating our faith in God's mighty works on his people's behalf. Similarly there is a quality of praise and thanksgiving in the way the creed formulates our faith in God. In particular our creed, as a Trinitarian act, helps to bring into focus the God towards whom our Eucharistic worship will be directed: God the Father, to whom we offer; God the Son, whom we offer; God the Holy Spirit, at whose inspiration we offer. This is perhaps the reason why, in some of the Eastern liturgies, the creed comes immediately before the Eucharistic Prayer.

The Bidding Prayers

This part of the Mass is referred to as 'the Prayer of the Faithful' or 'the General Intercessions' or 'the Bidding Prayers.' Solemn public intercession at the conclusion of the liturgy of the word is one of the elements that goes back to the synagogue. From there it passed into early Christian liturgy. We read of it already in the middle of the second century in Rome: 'We all rise up together and offer prayers' (St Justin). At one

stage these petitions took the form of a litany with a repeated
Kyrie eleison as a response. This prayer was later moved to its
present position, where its full significance was lost. The
restoration of the intercessions to the conclusion of the liturgy
of the word is one of the reforms called for by Vatican II itself
(*Liturgy Constitution,* art. 53). This text of the council conveys
something of the spirit of the prayer and is even sometimes
seen to suggest a structure for the petitions:

> By this prayer, in which the people are to take part,
> intercession will be made for holy Church, for the civil
> authorities, for those oppressed by various needs, for all
> humankind, and for the salvation of the entire world.
> (cf. 1 Tim 2:1-2)

One writer made the point more forcefully: the prayer 'is
pitifully misunderstood when it functions as a rehash of the
sermon, a bulletin-board for parish activities, or a catalogue of
our pet projects'.[3]

In many places in the early Church, this prayer came only
after the catechumens had been dismissed. It is a case of 'the
faithful,' the community of the baptized, priest and people
alike, exercising the common priesthood we all have from our
Baptism, interceding for the Church and the world. It is one of
the most solemn exercises of petition in the liturgy. Petitions
are formulated at other stages of the Mass, not least in the
Eucharistic Prayer itself, but this is the main act in the liturgy
entirely given over to the prayer of petition.

One of the great challenges for anyone responsible for
liturgy is to ensure that the life of the local community finds
expression in the liturgy. The Prayer of the Faithful is one of

---

3. *Christ in Sacred Speech,* G. Ramshaw Schmidt, Philadelphia 1986, p. 98.

the points where this requirement is especially relevant. Some imagination is needed to bring out something of the local situation without necessarily trivializing the prayer in the manner described above. I have a very vivid memory of the parish in Africa where I used to celebrate Mass. This parish was divided into a number of very active small Christian communities among the very poor. Every Sunday the presentation of the Prayer of the Faithful was assigned to different communities in turn, from whom a group would appear proudly at the altar with a microphone to lead the congregation in the prayers they had themselves composed. Apart from the excellence and fervour of their petitions, the very movement of people helped us avoid any sense of routine.

> *Blessed are those who hear the word of God and keep it.*
> (Lk 11:28)

8   THE LITURGY OF THE EUCHARIST

From time immemorial the Jewish people have had a rich tradition of worship in the home. Not only were the various feast-days marked by special prayers and rituals, but even each working day had its share of sacred customs of various kinds. In particular there were a number of traditional rituals when the family sat down to table together. It is a common view among scholars today that it was in adapting these familiar rituals to his own purposes at the Last Supper that our Lord gave the liturgy of the Eucharist to the Church.

Grace at Table
Amongst the Jews every family meal began with what we would call 'grace before meals'. With the Jews, however, it was not simply a prayer. It was a brief ritual, comprising both words

and gestures, and these were carried out according to certain traditional patterns and rubrics. Whoever presided over the meal would take bread, cover it with a napkin, and over it he would pray somewhat as follows:

> Blessed are you, Lord our God, King of the universe – you bring forth bread from the earth.

At these words the bread would be uncovered, raised up before God and then broken and distributed to those present.

Grace after meals was a ritual over wine. It was a slightly longer ceremony and it was usually celebrated only on special days, for instance on sabbath days and on feast-days. After some preliminary prayers, with responses from those present, the head of the household would raise in his right hand a cup of wine. He would first bless God for the food he gives us. Then, after pouring in some water, he would thank God for his goodness in the past and would go on to pray for his continued protection and mercy in the time to come. Then all present would conclude by drinking some wine.

These ancient table rituals are observed in Jewish homes to this day. We cannot be certain that all the present words and rubrics date back to the time of our Lord, but the general style and structure of the ritual is more than likely the same as in his day. The relevance of all this for our purposes is that, when our Lord came to establish the Eucharist, he did not start from zero. At the Last Supper there would have been grace before and after meals, as on any festive occasion. It is reasonable to hold that our Lord took these rituals and celebrated them in a new way, relating them to the mystery of his death and resurrection.

The Text of the Prayers
As regards the texts themselves, a certain liberty seems to have been customary from the beginning, once one stayed within

the traditional structure. On feast-days the content of the prayers could be made to refer to the subject-matter of the particular feast. At Passover, for instance, each of the blessings after the meal would be expanded to include references to the Exodus of the people in the time of Moses, when they escaped from Egypt to the promised land. In this kind of tradition it is easily understandable how in these prayers at the Last Supper our Lord would have spoken of his own 'exodus', that is to say of his own passage from this world to the Father in the mystery of his death and resurrection.

The Outer Form

In describing these table rituals out of which our Eucharist comes, we are still only on the outside of things. We are merely talking about the external form of the Eucharist and seeing what a simple ritual it really is. What gives the Eucharist its unique value comes from our Lord's filling these rituals with the presence of the Holy Spirit and so binding them to the mystery of his death and resurrection. As we shall see, the key thing in the Eucharist is not its outer form but its inner content, and that inner content is nothing less than the mystery of Christ's death and resurrection renewed among us.

At the same time it is helpful to relate the outer form of the Eucharist to its humble origins in the table rites of the Jews. In the course of time, when celebrating this liturgy in the way our Lord had requested at the Last Supper, the early Christians brought the two rituals over bread and cup together and fused them into one; and the various prayers over the elements became the canon of the Mass. As a result our liturgy of the Eucharist today is made up of four main parts:

- the Preparation of the Gifts,
- the Canon or Eucharistic Prayer,

- the Breaking of the Host,
- the Communion,

each part reflecting an action of our Lord at the Last Supper:

> he took bread and wine;
> he blessed God over them;
> he broke the bread;
> he gave Holy Communion to his disciples.

In the following chapters of this section we will go through each of these main parts of the Eucharist in turn, examining their component words and rites one after the other, but before taking up that task in the next chapter, there are three final reflections to be made on the subject-matter of this one.

Simple Homely Things

When our Lord came to give his community its central act of worship, it is remarkable that he took its outward form not from the sacrificial cult of the Temple with all its pomp and circumstance, but rather from the familiar table rituals of the Jewish home. This act of worship was indeed to be sacrificial, but it will be a new, more spiritual, sense of sacrifice, and that aspect will be based, not on its outer form, but on its inner content. These simple acts of grace before and after meals, which we have described, were to become the vehicle of the great act of worship which the cross of Calvary would establish at the centre of the Christian community.

In this way our Lord is telling us something about Christian life and worship. First of all we see here something of our Lord's love of simplicity. That same simplicity which astounds us in the manger astounds us in the Mass. Our Lord does not come to startle and overwhelm us with a display of the power and magnificence which is his right. He comes to us rather in a lowliness greater than our own, because he wants us to feel able to be close to him.

The Divine Initiative

But there is an even deeper reason for our Lord's turning away from the forms of Temple cult. This custom of cultic sacrifice is part of the universal tradition of human religion by which, out of the depths of human nature, human beings seek to find their way to God. Revealed religion, however, begins from above, not from below. It arises out of God's search for human beings, not out of our search for God. The context of table fellowship, brought before us by our Lord's choice of external form of his worship, fits in better with this gospel notion of God taking the initiative in inviting us all to his table (cfr Lk 14:15-24).

Liturgy and Life

But what is perhaps even more important, our Lord is telling us something about the relationship of liturgy to life. In avoiding the ceremonial of the Temple and in leaving aside the elaborate ritual of the Passover Meal, our Lord seems to be directing our attention to where the true value of liturgy lies. The value of our liturgy depends on the quality of our Christian living. Already the rituals of the Jewish grace at table were simply rituals of consecration, which called down God's blessing on the meal and on all who shared in it. In the Eucharist there is, strictly speaking, no meal, at least not in the physical sense of the term. A piece of a wafer and a sip of wine do not constitute a meal in any ordinary sense of the word. Of the original meal we retain only the two simple rituals of consecration. Life itself is the meal. In the Mass we consecrate and offer to God the life we live every day. We offer it through, with and in the offering of Christ on the Cross brought before the people by the rituals of his supper; but unless we give meaning to our offering by the way we live our lives, then our

Mass cannot be fruitful and our protestations of love are no better than sounding brass and tinkling cymbal.

> *The Church is especially concerned that the faithful not attend this mystery of faith as outsiders or silent spectators, but that, being led by the rites and prayers to a good understanding of what is going on, they may participate in the sacred action knowingly, prayerfully and actively.*
>   Vatican II

9   THE PREPARATION OF THE GIFTS

The points made at the end of the preceding chapter make a good introduction to the part of the liturgy to which we have now come, for the whole issue before us at this stage of the celebration is precisely that of ensuring that we put meaning into our Mass.

Preparation is here the keynote, as the name of this part of the Mass implies. While the priest and his helpers prepare our gifts at the altar, we should prepare ourselves for the offering that is to follow. We need to reflect on the things being prepared and by our thoughts to make them our own. They are to be our gifts, standing for our lives before God. As host and cup will be transformed into Christ's body and blood, so we should intend to offer to God our very selves, that our lives might be transformed into what he wants them to be. Bread and wine stand for the whole of our existence, which we wish to bring to God. The bread, in a special way, can stand for our labour, by which we earn our daily bread. Wine, the noblest of our festive drinks, can stand for the joys of life, which also come from God and should be returned to him. In an especially vivid way, the drop of water into the cup stands for us, the people, dropped into the wine of Christ's mystery and so destined to be brought by him before the Father.

This part of the Mass has gone through much development ever since that night when our Lord took the bread and cup into his hands at the Last Supper. Prior to Vatican II, this section of the liturgy was referred to as 'the Offertory,' but, apart from the expression 'Offertory Procession,' the new liturgy prefers the more modest title 'Preparation of the Gifts,' which gives a better clue to its meaning. To speak of the Offertory often gave the impression that here we have an offering of bread and wine prior to the offering of Christ's body and blood in the canon. Nothing could be further from the truth. In the New Law there is only one offering, that of Christ's body and blood, as the Letter to the Hebrews makes clear. There is then no room for a little Jewish offering of bread and wine prior to the one great sacrifice of Christ brought before us in the Eucharistic Prayer. The moment of offering and the prayer of offering have to wait, as we will see, for the canon of the Mass.

Presenting Host and Cup

A Gospel parallel, which might help us to enter into the spirit of this part of the Mass, is that story about the people bringing bread and fish to the apostles in the desert, who then presented them to Christ for him to work the miracle of multiplication (Mt 14:18). Similarly in the Mass the bread and wine are brought to the priest who then presents them to the Lord. The prayers he now uses are very simple ones, modelled on Jewish blessings: 'Blessed are you, Lord, God of all creation...' In a Jewish festive meal, as in the Passover, there are some brief preliminary blessings and rituals before one comes to the main meal. Our rituals at the presentation of the gifts are something like that, leaving to the Eucharistic Prayer the great theme of our offering united with that of Christ, but they look forward to that great moment of worship when they speak of our bread becoming 'the bread of life' (Jn 6:35), and the cup becoming 'our spiritual drink' (1 Cor 10:4), namely a drink that works through the Holy Spirit.

Rite of Mingling

In almost all the great liturgies of Christendom the Eucharistic cup is prepared by mixing water with the wine. This practice is so widespread in the liturgy because it goes back to the Jewish origins of our rites, where the cup of blessing at the end of the meal was always a mingled cup. The reason for the custom is not entirely clear. Some think it may be purely practical, since the wine of Palestine tended to be somewhat thick. In Christianity, however, the addition of the water to the wine has always been seen as richly symbolic. On one level it recalls the union of divine and human in Christ, as the prayer accompanying the gesture suggests. On another level, the water, as sign of Christ's humanity, also recalls the humanity of all of us, united with his in the one body of the people of God. Already in the third century, St Cyprian (d. 258 AD) saw in the practice this union of Christ with his Church. Since Vatican II, the medieval custom of first blessing the water has been abandoned. This return to an earlier simplicity is a way of saying that the things of creation are good and have no need to be made holy by a blessing before coming on to God's table.

Washing of Hands

Once again we meet a practice which is found in every liturgy and so must go back to the very origins of our worship. In fact a ritual washing before prayer is an ancient tradition of middle-Eastern peoples generally, found both in Judaism and in Islam. It is an act of reverence before entering into God's presence. Among Christians it inevitably recalls the way our Lord gave it special emphasis by washing the feet of his disciples at the Last Supper. It is thus part of the whole memorial of that night on which the Mass began. The accompanying verse from Ps 50(51) interprets the rite as a prayer for inner purification. People in medieval times often thought that the custom had something to do with Pilate's washing of his hands at the trial of Jesus, but the history we have just described shows that this view is mistaken.

The Offertory Procession

Sometimes the message of this part of the Mass is dramatized in a most striking way by an offertory procession. This practice has a long history, going back at least to the third century, when the people themselves used to bring to the church the bread and wine used at the Mass. It was a time when people were becoming more conscious of how our worship is rooted in the things of creation, and so they became anxious to bring more clearly into the worship of the Creator a joy in the things he had made, for 'God saw all the things that he had made and they were very good' (Gen 1:31). With this kind of thought in mind, people today often extend the signs of bread and wine by bringing up other gifts as well: flowers and lights to express the beauty of creation, objects of familiar usage to express our daily lives, gifts of food and drink to remind us of our obligation to the poor.

In my experience the experts in offertory processions are African Christians, who have an innate sense of the joy of celebration. I remember in particular the offertory procession in Congo-Kinshasa, where, on an ordinary Sunday, the procession would be formed of up to a dozen people, dressed in colourful clothes, bearing various gifts, moving up to the altar from the heart of the congregation in a vibrant but dignified rhythmic movement, with the whole church singing and clapping with the accompanying music. This was truly an act of the whole people, and there was no room for complaints about being 'bored' at Mass!

Prayer over the Gifts

There are three rites of movement in the Mass, the entrance procession, the offertory procession and the distribution of holy communion. Each of these movements ends in a solemn presidential prayer, the collect, the prayer over the gifts and the post-communion. In the early liturgy, the prayer over the gifts was the only prayer assigned to the celebrant during the preparation of the bread and wine. This he carried out, and continues to carry out, in his capacity as representing the Church: he receives the gifts on behalf of the Church and of Christ, and through the prayer assigns them their place in our sacrificial worship; but before he does so, he first asks the people's permission when he addresses them, 'Pray, brethren,' (*Orate fratres*) and they respond accordingly. All this gives to this moment of prayer a particular solemnity. The style of the prayer, and many of the actual texts in our missal, are in keeping with this spirit, since they come down to us from the renown masters of prayer of the ancient Roman Church of Leo the Great (d. 461 AD) and Gregory the Great (d. 604 AD).

The Collection
There is one final act of this part of the Mass which remains to be described, one that in fact sums up in a very practical way a lot of the themes we have just been considering. I refer to the collection. Ever since our Lord drove the traders from the temple, Christians will easily tend to be suspicious of the chink of money around the altar. As a result we often regard the collection as little better than a regrettable necessity, realizing as we do that there is nothing free in life, not even the organization of churches and liturgies; but this is to fall well below the way this act was understood by the first Christians. For them it was an essential part of Christian cult, belonging to that common sharing of goods and sacrificial giving which is what the Eucharist is all about.

One place where that becomes very clear is in the ministry of Paul who often writes about the collection which he wants to take up in Rome and in Corinth for the Christians of Jerusalem (1 Cor 16:1-3). It comes out particularly in the terms which he applies to the collection. They are taken from some of the most sacred terms in the vocabulary of Christian cult. He calls it *koinonia*, which is the word for 'sharing' or 'communion' (Rom 15:26), and also *diakonia*, the word for 'service' (2 Cor 9:1). In this way it appears that the collection is not a purely profane act but is part of that evangelical holding of goods in common which was one of the features of early Church life (Acts 2:44-46). It can also be seen as part of that sacrificial giving to others in service which was to be the mark of Christians. When we reflect that the Eucharist is the sacrifice of our Lord's self-giving, then some gesture of giving that hits our pockets is one of the most immediate and obvious signs that we really mean what we say when we prepare to take part in this worship.

> *They said to him, We have here only five loaves and two fish, and he said, Bring them to me.*
>   (Mt 14:18)

10   THE CANON OF THE MASS

The great Prayer of Offering in the Mass is the Eucharistic Prayer, traditionally called 'the Canon of the Mass' in the West, and in the East 'the Anaphora' (literally, the 'offering'). In the official introduction to the Roman Missal, this prayer is described as 'the climax and very heart of the entire celebration.' The canon and holy communion belong together as the two most important parts of the entire liturgy of the Mass. In the Eucharistic Prayer, not only is the prayer of the local congregation drawn into that of the whole Church, but at the consecration the voice of the priest melts into that of Christ himself.

Prior to Vatican II this section of the missal had the Latin words *canon actionis* as its heading, which might be translated 'the order of the action.' The title has the advantage of underlining that this part of the Mass is more than just the communal reciting of a prayer. It is an *action*, the core of the Eucharistic action. Something more fundamental is going on in the canon of the Mass than simply our offering a prayer to God, great as that prayer is.

The Eucharistic Action
The Eucharistic Prayer is an act of worship. For us it is the door by which we enter into the great mystery of worship which is the central action of the Mass. Since Christ is the High Priest of all humanity, it is not surprising that it is an act of worship which should open up for us our entrance into the mystery in the heart of Christ in every Mass. As we will see, the Eucharistic Prayer has a number of parts and standard themes, but all of them are one in being part of this one great act of worship, which lies behind all we say and do in the Mass.

In its outward form the Eucharistic Prayer is the Church's act of worship. In its inner content it is that and something more: it is the great act of worship and self-oblation, which is carried out by Christ himself in every Mass, and by us with him and in him. Here at the high point of our liturgy we acknowledge our incapacity of worshipping God on our own. Through the Eucharistic Prayer we enter into the heart of Christ, so that our worship might pass into his, and his great act of love and surrender may carry ours before the Father. The key expression for what we do at Mass is not just to hear Mass or to assist at Mass but to offer Mass, or, more exactly, to offer Christ to the Father, ourselves in him and our lives in his life.

This part of the Mass is one of those four main acts of the Eucharist which go back to our Lord himself at the Last Supper. After taking bread and wine, he carried out the blessing over each of these elements. This does not mean that he made the sign of the cross over them. 'Blessing' here refers to a prayer of thanksgiving and praise with which he blessed his Father for the goodness of his providence. More than once the New Testament attributes this form of prayer to our Lord (e.g. Mt 11:25-27; Lk 10:21). The outstanding instance is John chapter 17, which has been referred to as the 'high priestly prayer' of Christ. We cannot be sure of the exact words of our Lord's Eucharistic Prayer at the Last Supper, but we can reasonably take it that it was something like this prayer in John 17, at least in general style if not also in content.

A Great Symphony

The story of Christ's worship of the Father is like a great symphony in which the one basic theme of Christ's great act of worship is played out in four different movements. The first movement can be located at the Last Supper, where Christ reveals the attitude of worship and surrender with which he faced into the day which lay ahead. In the second movement that same theme returns but in the minor key of his final tragedy, in which his inner attitude transforms Calvary into the great act of sacrificial worship which redeems the world. The third movement takes up the same theme again but this time with a note of triumph and joy, as Christ's act of worship comes to its fulfilment in the liturgy of heaven. The fourth movement is the Eucharist, and the theme is found especially in the Eucharistic Prayer. Here, in the humble circumstances of local churches everywhere, the same theme of Christ's worship and surrender is celebrated still, as our worship is transformed into Christ's, in union with the Last Supper, with Calvary and the liturgy of heaven.

The Form of the Prayer

Most of us probably take the Eucharistic Prayer for granted, but at some point in the past, before the shape of the liturgy had become clear, the question had to be raised as to what would be an appropriate form of words with which to accompany Christ's great act of worship in the Mass. The answer to that question came out of the tradition of Jewish prayer such as we find it in the great prayers of the Bible. Some scholars even take the view that the Eucharistic Prayer was modelled on the Jewish grace after meals. If this view can be accepted, then we have another reason for seeing our Eucharist in continuity with the rite our Lord used at the Last Supper. In what follows we will take our cue from this approach.

Our form of the Eucharistic Prayer begins with the dialogue before the preface and ends with the Amen before the 'Our Father'. This dialogue is one of our links with the Jewish grace after meals, since it too began with a similar interchange. Then we have the preface. This preface is not a kind of introduction but is an integral part of the whole prayer. The word 'preface' here does not mean 'speech before the main part' but 'speech out loud' or 'speech before other people.'

Three Movements
The prayer can be divided into three main parts or movements, each of them corresponding to the three sections of the Jewish grace after meals. The first part is an act of praise and thanksgiving, in which we join ourselves to the whole body of Christ, and in particular to the heavenly liturgy of the angels and saints. This part concludes with the people's acclamation, 'Holy, Holy, Holy' according to the model of the heavenly liturgy revealed in the Bible (Is 6:3; Apoc 4:8).

The second part is a commemoration of salvation history. Sometimes this can be protracted as in our Canon IV, sometimes it can be very brief as in Canon II, but always it includes the recital of our Lord's own words about his sacrifice in body and blood on the cross. In this way our Lord's act of worship on the cross is seen to be the pivot of our worship as it is the pivot of every

Eucharistic Prayer. It is worth noting that the acclamation after these words about our Lord's sacrifice is always followed by a prayer of offering, inviting us to offer our lives in union with his.

The third movement of the canon is that of petition and intercession. Though sometimes as in Canon I (the Roman Canon) this can occur both before and after the consecration, more usually it comes after the recital of Christ's sacrifice, with the request that it bear fruit in the life of the Church through the intercession of the saints. The Eucharistic Prayer then comes to an end in its final expression of praise and thanksgiving, 'through him, with him, in him ...' To this the people reply with their Amen, sometimes called the Great Amen, since it is the most solemn Amen of the Mass. By it the people set their seal on the great act of worship which Christ and his Church have just carried out on their behalf.

Learning to Pray the Canon
To follow the canon of the Mass in a prayerful and attentive spirit is a skill to be taught and learned. In the liturgy prior to Vatican II, when most of the canon was in silence, people learned to follow it with silent adoration, focusing especially on the advent of Christ at the consecration. Today they will need more direction and information, such as that outlined in the preceding paragraphs. Their attention might be drawn to particular evocative phrases, which can be like pegs on which to hang our prayer: phrases like 'to grow in love', 'make us an everlasting gift to you,' 'that we might live no longer for ourselves but for him'. But more importantly I would like to suggest that they be made more aware of the three basic movements of this prayer with which they should be invited to identify themselves.

Praise, Offering and Petition
The first movement of the Eucharistic Prayer is one of praise and thanksgiving for redemption. Often our prefaces focus on

one particular aspect of God's redeeming work, but behind it
all and source of it all is the loving mercy of the heart of God,
to which we can respond only by thanksgiving. A key text here
is John 3:16, 'God so loved the world that he sent his only
begotten Son.' The human race was a race of sinners, enemies
of God, but God loved his enemies, not because we were
lovable, but because he first loved us (1 Jn 4:10). God's gift of
his Son in our redemption is mirrored in the way he gives us his
Son in the Eucharist. This is where it all begins, in the heart of
God, and all we can do is to say, Thank-you, which is what we
do at the beginning of every Eucharistic Prayer.

But thanksgiving can be an ambiguous prayer, as our Lord
himself indicates (Mt 7:21; Lk 18:9ff), if it is not rooted in
commitment to God's will. This concern brings us into the
second movement of the Eucharistic Prayer in which we
commit ourselves to the will of God by offering our very selves
to Him. This is something which neither we nor the Church
can do on our own, and so we turn to the self-offering of Christ
on the cross, which we here remember and make present
among us as we join our offering to his.

By a natural progression this concern gives way to one
about the fruitfulness of our worship (cfr Jn 15:8), and so the
entire third movement of the prayer, with all its intercessions,
is most fittingly placed under the patronage of the Holy Spirit,
whose role it is to bring the work of Christ to completion. This
part of the prayer, then, is a petition to the Holy Spirit that our
Mass may be fruitful, not only for ourselves but for all those for
whom we now intercede.

The Heavenly Liturgy
Finally we might notice that the real setting of the Eucharistic
Prayer is the liturgy of heaven and the triple throne at its
centre. The words of our prayers might have been made on

earth, but the worship they celebrate is made in heaven, and every Eucharistic Prayer marks the response of those in heaven, on earth and under the earth to the self-gift of each of the three divine persons, each in their different ways.

> *The meaning of this prayer is that the whole congregation of the faithful unites itself with Christ in praising the mighty deeds of God and in offering the sacrifice.*
> The Roman Missal

11   PREPARATION FOR HOLY COMMUNION

On the conclusion of the canon of the Mass the liturgy enters a new preparatory stage as the assembly gets ready for the next highpoint of the liturgy, namely holy communion. This third of the four main parts of the Eucharist can be broken up as follows:

1)   the 'Our Father'
2)   the Sign of Peace
3)   the Breaking of Bread
4)   the Mingling of the Species
5)   Prayers before Communion.

The 'Our Father'
Among all the words of the New Testament, those of the Our Father are second in importance only to those used by our Lord at the institution of the Eucharist. Here we have our Lord's own lesson on prayer, in which he invites us to learn by doing. In most Eastern liturgies the Our Father has always occurred at this point in the Mass, but in the West it has been placed here only since the time of Gregory the Great. He wanted to bring the sacred text of Christ's prayer as close as possible to the newly consecrated Eucharistic gifts, in order, as he tells us, to

pray the prayer of the Redeemer over the body and blood of the Redeemer.

In a sense the Our Father is a confirmation of the Eucharistic Prayer by the entire congregation. It is a similar kind of prayer, coming out of the same tradition of Jewish prayer. It opens with adoration and closes with petition, the adoration-part corresponding to the praise and thanksgiving of the Preface, the petition-part corresponding to the intercessions in the canon. The central phrase of the Our Father is the great declaration in which adoration, petition and oblation are fused into one: *Thy will be done.* In this phrase we come close to our Lord's great act of self-oblation in Gethsemane, 'Not my will but thine be done.' By this phrase we confirm the offering of ourselves made already in the Eucharistic Prayer.

But in the liturgy the Our Father also looks forward to that which lies ahead. It is our introduction to the third main part of the Eucharist which is our preparation for Holy Communion. The Our Father has been described as the Prayer of the Kingdom, because it expresses in particular the sense the early Christians had that the kingdom of God was breaking in upon them. There is something of that same sense in the rite of holy communion, since the Eucharist, as will be explained later, is a foretaste of that banquet of the kingdom which our Lord seems to have had in mind at the Last Supper (Mt 26:29). In this context it is interesting to notice how many times the kingdom is mentioned in the Mass from the Our Father on:

a)   thy kingdom come
b)   for the kingdom, the power and the glory are yours
c)   the peace and unity of your kingdom
d)   bring eternal life (= kingdom)
e)   who are called to his supper (= kingdom)
g)   bring me to everlasting life (= kingdom).

In line with these thoughts we can see the Our Father in the Mass as the prayer of Christ's little flock, awaiting the great things which God has planned for us. It is a prayer with a deep sense of dependence and human frailty, standing humbly under God's power, but sustained by confidence in God our Father (cfr Mt 7:9-11). We notice that the prayer is in the first person plural. It is the voice of the Christian community, giving expression to the new being we have as sons and daughters of God, 'sons in the Son,' presuming to call God Father, Abba, in Jesus' own inimitable way. We should notice in particular the petition for our daily bread, since these words have commonly been understood by the early saints as a reference to the bread of the Eucharist as well as to our ordinary food. The bread of the Eucharist is the bread of the kingdom which will be fulfilled one day in the kingdom of heaven (cfr Lk 14:15).

The Sign of Peace
One of the unforgettable words of our Lord in the Gospel is that in Mt 5:23-24,

> If you are offering your gift at the altar, and there you remember that your brother has something against you, leave your gift there before the altar; go and be reconciled to your brother first, and then come and offer your gift.

This command has weighed heavily on Christians from the beginning. It is clear that for our Lord the spirit of forgiveness is to be one of the hallmarks of his disciples, and this teaching in Mt 5 has linked the point forever with the liturgy.

The custom of greeting one's fellow Christians with a liturgical kiss seems to go back to the New Testament itself, as we see from the conclusion of Paul's letters (Rom 16:16; 2 Cor 13:12). Following that precedent, but also with Mt 5:23 in mind, the usual place for this gesture is at the conclusion of the liturgy of the word. However, in the Western liturgy, it has long been seen as an extension of the prayer for forgiveness in the Our Father. One early writer called the kiss of peace 'the seal' on our prayer, and this expresses very well how it belongs so closely to the petition for forgiveness in the Our Father. Augustine once asked the question, 'Who would not be angered seeing brother plot against brother, breaking faith with the kiss they imprint in God's sacraments?' Of course the gesture does not always take the form of a kiss. Differences of time and place can play a role, but the important thing is surely having some act to show that our union with Christ in the sacrament presupposes our respect for those around us in daily life.

The Breaking of Bread
One of the great scenes of the Gospel, one that has appealed to our greatest artists, is certainly that in the inn at Emmaus, as the voice and hands of Jesus hold the attention of the two disbelieving disciples, so that it finally dawns, even on them, that Jesus is risen and is present before them. There was something of the uniqueness of Jesus in that action of the breaking of bread. In our liturgy this same rite remains as one of its most meaningful acts. It sums up in a gesture one of the special concerns of Christ, namely that this sacrament is to form the unity of Christians: We, being many, are one body, because we all share in the one bread, which is Christ himself (cfr 1 Cor 10:16-17). An early Christian writing put it like this:

> Just as the grains of wheat, scattered on the mountains, were gathered together and became one loaf, so will your Church be gathered from the ends of the earth into your kingdom.
> (The Didaché)

After the New Testament Christians came to see in the breaking of the host a reminder of the breaking of Christ's body on the cross. This seems to be the inspiration behind the chant, 'Lamb of God,' which is the people's way of accompanying the ritual. The gesture also evokes the memory of the multiplication of the loaves, but now it is our Lord, out of love for each of us, multiplying the fullness of his presence in every fragment of the sacrament. With all this significance in the rite one can see how desirable it is that this simple gesture be carried out on its own in a deliberate and solemn way, so that the ritual can stand out and be visible to all.

The Placing of the Rite
In all the liturgies the breaking of the host comes after the Eucharistic Prayer. This corresponds to the original sequence, for our Lord first prayed his blessing-prayer to the Father before going on to break the host. However, since the description of that first Eucharist is now incorporated into the Eucharistic Prayer, there is a mention of the breaking in every canon. This has suggested to some a gesture of breaking the host already within the Eucharistic Prayer, but this is based on several false ideas.

For one thing, it fails to take account of the way the Lord's original words and gestures have had to be re-arranged somewhat to suit the circumstances of our liturgy. In fact, within those limits, our arrangement is actually closer to the original than the innovation referred to above. Furthermore the ritual of breaking, being one of the most meaningful gestures of the liturgy, needs to be given a place of its own in the rite, lest it be overshadowed by the Eucharistic Prayer. One might also observe that those who favour breaking the host during the canon often have a notion of the liturgy as a kind of mime of the Last Supper. Even were they right in their view of the original sequence of events – which they are not – liturgy is not mime. It is a celebration of the meaning of what our Lord asked us to do, with a re-arrangement of the original actions in order to bring out their inner meaning for people who are not familiar with the original Jewish customs.

The Mingling

Immediately after the breaking of the host, there follows another ritual, which is so closely connected with what has gone before that it commonly passes unnoticed. It is the ritual of the mingling of a fragment of the broken host with the Lord's blood in the consecrated cup. This gesture is an ancient one, being spoken of already in the third century. It is one worth emphasising in catechising on the liturgy since it embodies a significant message.

From the times of the ancient Church, the separation of the Eucharistic species into two distinct kinds has been seen as a reminder of how Christ's body and blood were separated in death. Against this background one can appreciate the significance of reuniting the two species by dropping one part of the host into the cup. If the sundering of the sign is a symbol of Christ's death, the reuniting of the elements is a symbol of the resurrection. This is in fact the way the ritual is interpreted in the accompanying prayer when it prays for eternal life:

> May this mingling of the body and blood of the Lord
> bring eternal life to those who receive it.

Eternal life is the life that flooded back into our Lord's body at his resurrection, as it will one day be granted to all the friends of God in the resurrection from the dead. This ritual then suggests that the sign of Christ's death and resurrection is not found as fully in the host on its own as in host and cup together. However, as will be repeated later when we return to this subject, we must add an important point: in our Mass the 'separation' is only on the level of the sign; the reality in either species is that of the risen Christ, namely the whole Christ, as he is now in heaven, body, blood, soul, and divinity; and that is the reality we receive in either species.

Prayers before Communion

After the completion of the rites of breaking and mingling, a moment of quiet follows during which the celebrant prays one or other of two early medieval prayers. We might notice that these are an example of celebrant's prayers which are not presidential prayers. They are there to help the celebrants themselves, and so are said quietly. During these prayers, the people can pray these texts or others of their own choosing, but let us remember that the appropriate preparation for holy communion is not just one or other of such texts but our attentive participation in the whole ritual of the Mass which has gone before.

> One should examine oneself and so eat of that bread and drink of that cup, for those who eat and drink without discerning the body eat and drink judgment to themselves.
>   (1 Cor 11:28-29)

12   HOLY COMMUNION

Among the many ways that are open to us for active participation in the liturgy, first and foremost has to be our going to holy communion. It is the act which draws us most deeply into the mystery our Lord has left us, and it is the one which demonstrates most clearly our desire to enter into the Lord's self-offering for the sake of the world. The inner meaning of this ritual will be explored in later chapters of this

book. Here we will simply approach it in a preliminary way,
bearing in mind that it is one of the four main actions of the
Eucharist. After blessing and breaking, the Lord 'gave' the
disciples the consecrated gifts of his body and blood. Similarly
in the Mass he repeats that action through his ministers for the
benefit of us all.

The Great Banquet

Holy communion is the great banquet which the Lord has been
preparing for us since the beginning of the Mass. It is the same
Lord who once said that he would set before his people a great
banquet on the mountain of Sion at the end of time (Is 25:6-8).
Here now in the Mass we have a foretaste of that great day, as
the Lord sets before us a kind of first instalment of that final
rejoicing.

At Peace with God

But the Eucharist is a very special kind of banquet. It is the
conclusion of a sacrifice. In the Old Testament there were
communion sacrifices, where the eating and drinking of the
offerings was their way of showing the peace between God and
the people. Without that act the sacrifice was incomplete.
Similarly in every Mass the priest's communion is absolutely
required as the minimal sign of that peace; but everyone who
goes to communion becomes the bearer of that message on
behalf of all who go to Mass, whether these go to communion
or not.

A Communal Act

From these two aspects of the Mass we can draw two lessons
regarding the spirit in which to go to holy communion. Firstly,
as a sacred banquet, holy communion is not just something
between myself and 'my Jesus'. It is an act with other people, at

a common table with them, and so it engages us to a life of closer union with them. I cannot forget that in the same act in which the Lord shows his love for me he is also showing his love for those around me. This attitude should be reflected in the orderly manner with which people come up to communion. One of the better ways of expressing this in the liturgy occurs when all come up in the unity of a procession, preferably singing together a song that celebrates our union in Christ. The Communion Procession is one of the three standard rites of movement in the liturgy already referred to on a previous page.

A Sacrificial Act

Secondly, our sharing in the Lord's banquet is our communion in his sacrifice. Christ's body and blood had first to be 'given' on the cross before they could be 'given' in holy communion. Today we do not easily think of holy communion as a sacrificial act, but that is the meaning which St Paul had in mind when he compared holy communion to the way the people of Israel shared in the altar of God by eating the gifts which had been offered on that altar (1 Cor 10:18). Holy communion, therefore, is not a separate act from that of oblation in the Mass. It is rather an act by which we confirm in a solemn, public way our commitment to Christ's sacrifice and our desire, by deepening our union with him, to enter more fully into the movement of his self-offering.

The Distribution of the Sacrament

In recent years we have become more conscious of differences in the way the sacrament is distributed. Issues like communion in the hand, the use of lay-ministers, the abolition of kneeling, have all helped to make this act more obviously a moment of human fellowship as well as divine communion. Here only two observations will be made.

Firstly, it is important to see that, in the early tradition of liturgy, communion was always given by a minister. This is because the actual giving is part of the sacramental sign. The minister giving us host or cup is a sign of Christ giving us himself. Though sometimes when Mass is celebrated for a small group in a narrow space, the people might come up to take communion themselves, this should not be regarded as normal. Self-service liturgy is as out of place as the notion of self-service redemption.

Secondly, there is the question of communion in both kinds. A whole chapter will be devoted to this topic later in this book. There the suggestion will be made that we approach each kind in a different spirit. We might, for instance, approach the host as the bread of life, the source of that new life and strength which flows from Christ's incarnation and which we so badly need if we are to keep up living our lives in his image. The cup, then, can be received as the special gift of Christ's heart, the sign of that special love which he showed us on the cross, not least because of the blood flowing from his opened side.

Thanksgiving

The moments after holy communion are an especially sacred time in the movement of the liturgy, since it is an opportunity for drawing close to the Lord and resting in his presence. This is true for all who have celebrated the Lord's Eucharist, but especially for those who have received him in holy communion. One of the fruits of that gift is that the whole Trinity takes each of us to itself in a deeper way. St Cyril of Alexandria once said that, after holy communion, God is as closely united with each of us 'as wax with wax'.

How should we respond to that presence? The liturgy itself suggests that, where feasible, there should be a pause in the celebration and a few moments of silence be observed. It is at first surprising to learn that, for Vatican II, silence in the liturgy is a form of active participation (*Liturgy Constitution,* art. 30). Where the right atmosphere has been found, silence can become something you can almost touch. It binds people together and creates a time of communion amongst people as well as communion with God. We might learn from a proverb of the Kikuyu people in Kenya: 'Silence is thankfulness, a bounteous thing.'

It must be admitted that thanksgiving after communion has lost some ground in recent times. This is a great mistake since, unless we give time to such a practice, the miracle of God's closeness will lose its wonder and become for us a mere matter of routine. If we cannot do it fittingly during the Mass itself, then we should stay on afterwards for this unique moment of personal prayer. Sometimes people fill out this practice by reading some passages of scripture, for instance some verses from our Lord's discourse at the Last Supper in John's Gospel, chapters 14 to 17.

> *It is pleasant to spend time with him, to lie close to his breast like the Beloved Disciple (cf. Jn 13:25) and to feel the infinite love present in his heart.*
> (John Paul II)

13   THE CLOSING RITES

A Rite of Mission
The closing rites of the Mass are not to be lost sight of. They are brief, but not without their own meaning and solemnity. We could sum it up by saying that they are a rite of mission. By virtue of Baptism and Confirmation we all have a mission in life from God, and the Eucharist directs us along the path of that

mission to live out our Mass amongst the realities of everyday. St John Chrysostom once said that every street-corner and market-place is our altar. Teilhard de Chardin, the well-known scientist and philosopher, once found himself in the middle of a desert unable to say Mass. Instead, he tells us, he saw the whole world as his altar, on which he would offer to God all the labours and sorrows of the human race. He called it his 'Mass on the world.' These remarks remind us that, in a sense, ordinary life is still the Mass, in which the offering we made to God in the Mass is lived out in the divine presence, offered on the altar of the world. To continue offering Mass in the reality of daily life is the mission we carry out with us as we return to our homes.

The Notices

The closing rites are introduced with a simple act, which at first might seem to be purely practical, but which in fact acquires a certain significance from its official liturgical position at this point of the celebration. It is the reading of the notices about various events in the life of the local community. As the people prepare to return to their homes, the details of parish business remind them of the concrete context within which the life they have offered to God is to be lived. The celebrant may conclude this with a parting word, as St Augustine did on one occasion:

> You are about to go away, each to your own home. It was good to be together, good to have been glad together, good to have celebrated together; but as we depart from one another, let us not depart from God.[4]

The Solemn Blessing

Our celebration ends as it began with the invocation of the Trinity. Just as the Mass contains within itself the main point of

---

4.   Divine Office, Reading for Tuesday, Week 34.

the Gospel, so it ends in the way the Gospels end, namely with the mission of the Church to the world. The parallel between the Mass and the end of Matthew's Gospel is particularly close. There the risen Lord says to the disciples: 'Going therefore, teach all nations, baptizing them in the name of the Father and of the Son and of the Holy Spirit.' Similarly, at the end of the Mass, the priest, representing the risen Christ, recalls that mission which the people first received in Baptism by invoking on them the same holy Trinity, as they are sent out to take up their lives again.

Go, The Mass is Beginning

All these final words and gestures, then, are well summed up as a rite of mission. Sometimes the question is asked whether it is a good thing to go to Mass and communion more than once a day. The answer is, Normally no! Unless there is a special reason, such as a funeral or a wedding, once should be enough. The important thing, once the Mass is ended, is to go out and to live it!

The Mass on the World

As well as the Mass in the church, then, there is this 'Mass on the world,' and the first is really there for the sake of the second. Living the ups and downs of life in a spirit of faith is itself a form of worship, to be offered to God on the altar of the world (cfr Rom 12:1). Indeed living our lives in this spirit is really our way of living out the meaning of all we said and did when we were at Mass. It is an extension of the Eucharistic sacrifice into our everyday, as we offer to God the labour, joys and sorrows of the world. It can also be seen as an extension of Eucharistic presence, for we bring Christ with us out of the church to help build up his presence in the world. In both respects the Eucharist has given us a mission to extend the liturgy into life, and that is really the meaning of the closing acts of the Mass: to send the people out on this mission into the world, bringing with them on their way the blessing of the divine Trinity.

In the humble signs of bread and wine, changed into his body and blood, Christ walks beside us as our strength, and our food for the journey, and he enables us to become, for everyone, witnesses of hope.
(John Paul II)

PART II

UNDERSTANDING THE EUCHARIST

14   LIVING WITH MYSTERY

According to the liturgy itself the Eucharist is 'the mystery of
faith'. In our modern world we are not really used to mysteries,
since science seems to have an answer for everything. If we
come up against something we do not understand, we know
that there is always someone somewhere who has the answer.
It is just a matter of getting the right information and pressing
the right buttons.

But this is not the way with the Eucharist. The difference is
that here we are dealing with the things of God. Indeed the
mysteriousness of it all should be part of its attraction. St
Augustine (d. 430) once remarked about the divinity that, if we
understood him, he would not be God. The one thing a
preacher or teacher cannot say to us is, Sit down and I will
explain the Mass to you. No human being can 'explain' the
Mass in the sense of making it as plain as a pikestaff. The whole
point of approaching God through ritual is that we are reaching
beyond the range of our words and ideas and dealing with
realities about God and ourselves which we only half
understand. That is why we set words aside and turn to things
and gestures, to bread and wine and prayer, to offering,
adoration and communion. These external things reveal to us
something of the mystery, but there is a concealing in the
revealing, as there is a revealing in the concealing.

These remarks are made here by way of introduction to the second section of this book. This section is entitled 'Understanding the Eucharist,' but from the outset it must be clear that any understanding of a mystery will always be a limited one; and in the things of God, it is all the better for that! The really important things in life lie, not on the surface, but deep down, deeper than anything on which we can put a name. The Mass is one of the ways in which we get into touch with those deeper realities within us.

A Mysterious Doctrine

An outstanding example of this fact is found in one of the main points of doctrine about the Eucharist, transubstantiation. By this term we mean that, in the Eucharist, bread and wine are changed into the body and blood of Christ. The outer appearances remain the same, but the inner reality of either the bread or the wine is changed into the total reality of Christ's body, blood, soul and divinity. This is not an attempt to explain how the change comes about, but only to make clear what we mean by the change. The 'how' remains God's secret as much after as before. For us the only response is to believe it on his word: This is my body, this is my blood.

The Level of Faith

Often young people today complain that the Mass is boring. If the liturgy has been carried out in a wooden or unplanned way, they may have a point! But more often the real reason is something deeper. They come to church with the wrong expectation. They are used to going to pop-concerts, where no expense has been spared in overwhelming the audience with sound and sight and high-tech performance. There the whole thing is geared to immediate impact in the here and now. The liturgy cannot be like that.

Liturgy is part of faith, and faith is primarily not about the surface of life and impact in the here and now, but about the things which lie deep down, beneath the surface of events. That is where the really important things are, the long-term things, and that is the level which liturgy is designed to reach. In a youth-Mass it is obviously right to use the kind of music which appeals to young people, but even then there will always be a limit. The liturgy cannot rival a pop-concert, because it is about something else. It is not just about how we feel in the here and now, but about how we are before God, not only now but for the rest of our lives and for eternity.

Throwing a Little Light

Despite all this, mystery should not mean mystification. Though the Eucharist is indeed mysterious, that does not mean that something cannot be said about it. Within limits, we can understand a sacrament to some extent, and this is certainly a great help in learning to live with the mystery and to draw on the wealth of meaning it contains. This then is the main purpose of this section of the book, to throw at least a little light on the unsearchable riches of the Mass.

> The mystery of the Eucharist   sacrifice, presence, banquet –
> does not allow for reduction or exploitation; it must be
> experienced and lived in its integrity, both in its celebration
> and in the intimate converse with Jesus which takes place after
> receiving communion or in a prayerful moment of Eucharistic
> adoration apart from Mass.
> (John Paul II)

15 BROKEN BREAD

The Eucharist, as we have seen, owes its origin to what our Lord said and did at the Last Supper, but in trying to understand this sacrament it is helpful to see that particular occasion within a larger horizon. Indeed the Last Supper gets its meaning from a whole series of sacred events and signs, reaching back into the Old Testament on the one hand, and on into the future coming of the kingdom on the other.

The Banquet of Life

Perhaps its deepest inspiration comes from an image, first found in the prophets, where God's plan for the world is like that of a great king setting before all his people the great banquet of life. Immediately we think of our Lord's many parables on this theme. Again and again he spoke of his great goal in which we would all sit down with Abraham, Isaac and Jacob in the feast of the kingdom (Mt 8:11). This was his way of speaking of eternal life in heaven, and that is surely the end of it all, but we must not think that his meaning referred only to the next life. The banquet of life is also a statement about this world and about his plan for human relations here below. As Pope John Paul II expressed it in a recent encyclical, all human beings are to be made 'sharers on a par with ourselves, in the banquet of life to which all are equally invited by God' (*Sollicitudo rei socialis*, 39).

Seeing life here below as a great banquet underlines how everything we have and use in life is the gift of God's providence over us, for 'your heavenly Father knows that you have need of all these things' (Mt 6:32). This same way of looking at life throws light on why thanksgiving should be so central to Christian worship. At any meal the believer's first thought is to thank God for our nourishment. If, as was remarked in an earlier chapter, the whole of life is the meal set before us by God, then our most appropriate response of worship is like our grace before and after meals. In fact we have already seen how, in instituting the Eucharist at the Last Supper, our Lord took the Jewish way of saying grace before and after meals as the model for the external form of the Eucharist.

The Great Meals

If such is God's plan for the world, we can understand why so often great events of salvation take place in the form of a meal. In the time of Moses there was the gift of manna in the desert, with its lesson that we should depend on God for everything (Exod 16). Then there was the great day of the making of the Mosaic covenant, which ended with a mysterious meal when they ate and drank in the presence of God (Exod 24).

One of the first examples in the Gospels of Our Lord following in this tradition was his custom of eating and drinking with the outcast of society (cf. Mt 9:10-13). It was his way of revealing how God invites everyone to the table of salvation. When he fed the multitude in the desert, he was again pointing to the lavishness of divine generosity, of which he himself is to be the centre and the source (Jn 6:1-15). After the resurrection, in his meals with his disciples, he was pointing to the gatherings of his community as an anticipation of the final banquet in the feast of the kingdom (Lk 24:28-35; Jn 21:9-14). Running through all these events is the message that, in our being saved, it all begins with God. Salvation might require human effort, but first and foremost it is divine gift.

Sin Enters In

Seeing this line of sacred events and signs, we can understand why our Lord should turn to the notion of a banquet when he came to give shape and form to Christians' central act of worship. But the reality is not as straightforward as one might at first have thought. All we have said so far is very beautiful and positive and optimistic, but it leaves something out of account. So far we have been speaking of God's plan for the world and of what it would have been if it depended on him alone. But part of his plan was precisely that we should play a part in it. Human cooperation was to be central to it all, and that is where things begin to fall apart. In the actual course of human history there is the great wound of sin. Just as the main cause of famine in the world today is human warfare and mismanagement, so the main cause of the imperfection of the world is human selfishness and sin.

Christ's great vision for the world, where all humanity has its share in the banquet of life, does not come about automatically. There is not only the fact of real hunger and famine, but there is all the injustice and deprivation which manifest the reality of sin. If human beings are to overcome sin and selfishness, a painful process of withdrawal is necessary, withdrawing ourselves from the morass into which human sin has plunged the world. It is precisely because of the pain in such a process that Christ came to lead the way by his sacrifice on the cross. The answer to sin is Calvary. Just as Christ's heart was possessed by this vision of the banquet, he realized that it could be purchased only at a price. It is only through self-sacrifice that a new world can be born. It is only by dying to self that we can begin to give reality to the banquet Christ dreamed of. Not only is there the pain involved in withdrawing ourselves from our personal sins, there is also the necessary struggle against physical and spiritual hunger in the world, so that more and more people can have their fair share of the banquet of life.

Sacrifice and Banquet

The more you think about it, the clearer it becomes why the great celebration of Christian life, which Christ left us in the Eucharist, comes to us not in one image but in two. The Eucharist is not sacrifice alone; nor is it banquet alone; it is both sacrifice and banquet. At the Last Supper the disciples were engaged in celebrating the Passover sacrifice of their ancestors. The plotting of the leaders of the people to bring about our Lord's death was already under way. That was the very moment when our Lord chose to introduce the element of sacrifice into the great series of saving meals in which God's plan for the world is revealed. There is no community without self denial. There is no resurrection without the cross. There is no banquet without sacrifice. The image of the new creation is broken into two, sacrifice and banquet. The bread of life is a bread broken for a broken world.

A Lesson for Life

There is a lesson for life which follows from this, and it is one which we do not often associate with the Eucharist. If the Eucharist means sacrifice, then truly to celebrate it involves a commitment to union with Christ in his sacrifice. This does not mean simply drawing strength from him to accept the crosses of our personal lives – though it certainly means that too. The Eucharistic horizon is broader than that. When we think of the vision of the banquet for which Christ died, then it follows that we cannot be indifferent to the problems of our world where so many are excluded from the banquet of life. The Eucharistic person has to be concerned about such issues in our world. These are issues which weighed heavily on the heart of Christ in his time. If we are striving to be closer to him through the Eucharist, they must also be weighing on our hearts today.

> *At times one encounters an extremely reductive understanding of the Eucharistic mystery. Stripped of its sacrificial meaning, it is celebrated as if it were simply a fraternal banquet.*
> (John Paul II)

16   THE WORK OF THE SPIRIT

One of the abiding achievements of the Second Vatican
Council has been a growing appreciation amongst the faithful
of the significance of the Holy Spirit in the life of faith. It is
striking that in one of the first documents discussed by the
council, that on liturgy, comparatively little is said about the
Spirit. It was only as the council progressed, and in particular as
people became more aware of the Eastern Church, that the
appreciation of the place of the Spirit began to grow.
References to the Spirit are much more frequent in the later
documents of the council, and then in the new texts prepared
for the liturgy after the council there was a deliberate decision
to make more room for the role of the Holy Spirit. We can see
this, for instance, in the new canons of the Mass, particularly in
the Third Eucharistic Prayer; and in the fourth prayer the
overall task of Christ's Spirit is well described, 'To complete his
work on earth and bring us the fullness of grace.'

The Foundation of the Sacraments
The presence of the Holy Spirit is the fundamental reality in
the making of the Christian sacraments. More than once in this
book it has been remarked how, in founding the Christian
Eucharist, at least as regards its external form, Christ did not
start from nothing. Just as for Baptism he took the Jewish
custom of ritual washing and filled it with the Holy Spirit (Mk
1:8), so for the Eucharist he took the traditional ritual of grace
at table and filled it with the same Holy Spirit. In this way he
raised up these familiar rituals and gave them a totally new
meaning, placing them on a new plane altogether. In this way
the simple ritual of bread and cup became the central act of
worship in the new religion of humanity, filled with the
presence and power of the life-giving Spirit of God.

The Spirit and the Sacrifice

The role of the Holy Spirit in the Eucharist is mainly threefold. The first act of the Spirit provides a link between our liturgy and the role of the Spirit in the original sacrifice of Christ. We read in the New Testament that, on the cross, Christ was upheld by the presence of the Spirit in making his self-offering to the Father (Heb 9:14). In the Mass the same Holy Spirit is present to us in order to unite our offering today with that of Christ two thousand years ago; and one of the main ways he brings this about is by helping us to have the same mind which was once in Christ in his self-offering. If the Church can teach that the Mass is the same sacrifice as that of the cross, this can only be brought about through the presence of the timeless Spirit of God, who bridges the centuries and unites our worship with that of Christ and our minds and hearts with his.

The Spirit and the Change of our Gifts

The second task of the Spirit concerns our gifts of bread and wine, which are changed into Christ's body and blood. This change is associated in a special way with the work of the Holy Spirit in the Mass. Just as the third Person of the Trinity is the one who first formed the flesh and blood of Christ in the womb of Mary, so it is he who continues that role in bringing about that same flesh and blood in the mystery of the sacrament. An awareness of this grace has grown in the Western Church in recent times through our new Eucharistic Prayers. At one point in these prayers the Church solemnly prays that this change of our gifts may come about, and this petition is commonly entrusted explicitly to the care of the Holy Spirit. 'Let your Spirit come upon these gifts to make them holy, so that they may become for us the body and blood of our Lord Jesus Christ' (*Eucharistic Prayer* II).

The Spirit and the Church

Those who study these things, however, are anxious to point out that this change of our gifts is but part of a larger change which is also entrusted to the Holy Spirit. Here we recall the task of the Spirit to continue Christ's work on earth and bring it to completion. The main task for which the Spirit was sent at Pentecost was to build up the life of Christ in the faithful and so to complete the formation of that body which is his Church, preparing Christians for entering into the fullness of the Church at the end of time. The Eucharist is one of the main ways in which the Spirit brings this about; and if the Spirit changes our bread and wine into Christ's body and blood, this is but part of his design to change all of us who are nourished by this sacrament, bringing us all to enter into the attitudes of Christ's self-offering and so to become more fully members of his Church and part of his body in the world.

Elsewhere in this book we use the phrase, 'the Eucharist makes the Church.' Here we want to see that this 'making' of the Church is precisely the main task of the Holy Spirit in the sacrament. What it means is that the Spirit helps us to grow in love with God and with our fellow human beings, so that the unity and union, which are the special marks of Christ's kingdom, may be strengthened in our lives. One place where we might see this intention coming to the fore in a special way is in the intercessions of the Eucharistic Prayer. There we pray for union with all kinds of people, the Pope, the bishops, the saints, the dead, and all who seek God with a sincere heart. This prayer is the Eucharist making the Church, and it does that ultimately through the power of the Holy Spirit, whose presence is Christ's special gift to his Church.

> *We pray that you may send the Holy Spirit on the oblation of holy Church, that, bringing us into unity, you may grant that*

all who partake of these sacred things may be filled with the
Holy Spirit.

Ancient Eucharistic Prayer

17 EUCHARIST AND PASSOVER

The Church says extraordinary things of its Eucharist. It teaches that Christ makes present in the Mass the sacrifice of the cross, that he gives us his flesh to eat and his blood to drink, that the priest acts in the person and in the power of Christ himself. Now it is one thing for us to speak of these things today, for in believing them we have generations of faith behind us. But did it ever strike you how extraordinary it was for the early Christians to come to these beliefs in the first place? Indeed, how extraordinary that they should make any sense at all of what our Lord was saying to them!

One thing however which certainly helped them was the fact that they were Jews. From the wonder-filled history of their people they already knew something of the ways of God. Certainly, Christian truth is unique and goes beyond what is revealed in the Old Testament, but at the same time we must remember how the Old Testament was the providential preparation for the New.

The Passover is a good illustration of this. In the first three Gospels we are told that the Last Supper was a Passover. It is good to keep that in mind and to understand a little of what it means, for one of the ways the apostles came to understand what our Lord was doing in the Eucharist was to see that it was something like what Moses did when he established the Passover.

A Momentous Event
The Passover was one of the greatest of the Jewish feasts for it celebrated one of the greatest events of their history, the Exodus

of the people from Egypt. This event was the foundation event of the Jewish nation. It has been said that it did for the Jews what the struggle for independence in the eighteenth century did for the American people: it made them into a nation.

However, the Exodus was not only a political event. It did more than simply lay the foundations of the nation of Israel. It was a religious event also, and indeed that is its main significance. Being first and foremost an act of God, it was an extraordinary intervention of divine providence in human history, and it was not just in order to bestow political freedom, nor even simply freedom of worship. The freedom God gave his people in the Exodus was spiritual as well as political, internal as well as external. Not only did it bring freedom from Egypt; it also meant freedom from sin.

Always to be Remembered
The Exodus belongs to all Jews. As this event was the foundation grace out of which the identity of the Jewish nation has grown, so it has always had a meaning and a power for every succeeding generation of Jews. In the Passover liturgy we read:

> In every generation each one is bound to consider himself as having come out from Egypt, as the scripture says: And you will proclaim it to your son on that day, saying, 'This is what the Lord did for me when I came out of Egypt' (Exod 13:8). God the Holy One – blessed be he – redeemed not only our fathers, but he also redeemed us with them.

Moses established the Passover as the memorial of the Exodus:

> And this day shall be for a memorial to you, and you shall keep it a feast to the Lord in your generations with an everlasting observance (Exod 12:14).

In the first half of every Passover there was a long liturgy of the word, in which the ceremonies of the feast were explained and appropriate texts of scripture were recalled. The second half of the celebration was the paschal banquet. After grace had been said, the paschal lamb, which had been immolated in the temple earlier in the day, was consumed, in memory of the lamb that saved the Jews in Egypt (Exod 12:26f). Bitter herbs were eaten in memory of the bitterness of their slavery (Exod 1:14), and unleavened bread was taken as a sign of their haste in their flight from Pharaoh (Exod 12:39). The main meal was then concluded with the saying of grace over the final cup, which was called 'the cup of blessing'.

More than a Sign

The Passover was a vivid and moving ceremony. To this day it has a very special place in the hearts of Jews everywhere, but its place in Jewish life is not accounted for simply by the beauty of the texts nor the vividness of the ceremonial. Though it was a poignant sign of the Exodus, it was more than such a sign. In this memorial the events of the Exodus are not simply called to mind in a beautiful and nostalgic ritual. According to the traditional belief, these original events, in which the destiny of every Jew was involved, are made present and actual in a very real sense in the course of the liturgy. The Passover is no empty memorial of the Exodus. It might be called rather a *living* memorial, one filled with the reality of that which it commemorates, and the blessings of the Exodus come alive for the succeeding generations as they gather round the festive paschal table.

Light on the Mass

When we realize the very special kind of memorial which the Passover was for the Jews, we can see more clearly how the apostles would have understood our Lord at the Last Supper when he said, 'Do this in memory of me.' Our Lord also has events which he wants us to recall and relive in our liturgy, namely his own death and resurrection. These are his 'exodus', his passing over from this world to the Father, the foundation events of the new Israel. In Christ's death and resurrection the Church of the New Testament is born, and the blessings contained in these events are to be the source of Christian life ever afterwards.

If the sacrifice of the cross is Christ's 'exodus', the Mass is his 'Passover'. His words, 'Do this in memory of me,' take effect down through the centuries. The Eucharist is the memorial of his death and resurrection, but it is no empty memorial. Like the Passover of the Jews it is a living memorial, containing the reality of the events it commemorates. The Eucharist, then, is no mere passion play, no empty drama. It is a sacramental mystery in which the death and resurrection of Christ become actual in the midst of the celebrating community. It is, we have always said, the sacrifice of the cross, for it is the paschal mystery of Christ becoming alive for the people of God in our time.

> *This (the Passover Service) is no mere recitation of events that happened long ago and far away. We do not so much tell the story as re-enact it.*
> Rabbi Jonathan Sachs

18   SACRIFICE

Christianity is a sacrificing religion. To many of our contemporaries this will seem a surprising statement; but it still remains a fact of the Christian tradition, going right back to New Testament times, that sacrificial worship has a central place in Christianity. To sacrifice is one of the basic acts of humanity. The preservation of this act in the New Testament

brings home to us our Lord's understanding of human nature
and of how important it is that this most basic of human acts
should continue to have a place in his community.

Sacrifice, our catechism told us, is the first and most
necessary act of religion. By it we acknowledge God as our
Lord and Father, and we express our loving dependence on
him. This worship of the creator is the undertow of all religion,
and sacrifice is its most appropriate expression. By insisting on
the sacrificial aspect of the Eucharist we are bringing out how
the Eucharist is not only part of the mystery of redemption but
of that of creation as well. A religion without sacrifice is one
that is losing contact with its roots in creation and in the
mystery of being. Indeed this western world of ours is already
a world without roots. We are too sophisticated to
acknowledge the mystery in things, and so we are becoming
lost souls in the steel and concrete jungles of our own
technology.

Source and Goal

But what does it mean to offer a sacrifice? In itself it is a very
simple thing. To sacrifice is to give a gift to God as a sign of our
belonging to him. We give gifts to those we love at Christmas
and on birthdays. We make solemn presentations to important
people when we welcome them to our shores. Every week the
Christian people gathers to make a solemn presentation to God
to acknowledge him as the source and goal of our entire
existence.

In sacrifice, then, at least as it exists in the tradition of the
Bible, a gift is given to God. There is a transfer of ownership
over the offerings that are being presented at the altar. This
transfer is carried out as a sign of our belonging to God and of
our desire to give ourselves more completely to him. In the Old
Law this transfer of ownership took place when the gifts were

brought into contact with the altar in the Temple. In the Eucharist the transfer takes place in an unusual way when our offering is changed into the body and blood of Christ. Though different forms of sacrifice might signify the transfer in different ways, the basic message of worshippers everywhere remains the same: we belong to God and wish to belong to him ever more completely.

The Perfection of Sacrifice

In the Mass we have sacrifice in its most perfect form. It must be admitted, however, that in other times and places sacrifice has often been associated with some of the more unpleasant aspects of primitive religion. The institution of sacrifice had to undergo a long purification before it reached the purity and nobility which it has in the Mass. One point in particular is worth bringing to the fore.

In many primitive religions the divinity is understood to be a vengeful being. When the god has been angered by his worshippers, he must be placated in some way or he will punish those who have offended him. Ritual sacrifice has often been one of the ways of placating such gods and of averting their wrath.

Eucharistic sacrifice is not that kind of thing because our heavenly Father is not that kind of God. Christian sacrifice is different from other forms of sacrifice in that it begins and ends, not with human beings, but with God and with his love and mercy towards sinners. In the Eucharist the first to sacrifice is, in a sense, the Father himself, who did not spare his own Son but gave him up for us all (Rom 8:32; Jn 3:16). Our role in this sacrifice is entirely a matter of responding to what was started for us by the Father, manifested by the Son and destined to be completed by the Holy Spirit.

It is true that the sacrifice of the cross is an atoning sacrifice, and so the Eucharist has this aspect of atonement also. But it is in no sense the placating of a vengeful God. It is rather, on our part, the gesture of a loving sorrow, which is moved by the thought of God's mercy and by the memory of past offenses to ever greater demonstrations of its sorrowing love. It would make up for the past by some gesture in the present, much as the woman in the seventh chapter of St Luke's Gospel was stirred by the Pharisee's coldness to a special demonstration of her love; and as with the gesture of the repentant woman, the Eucharist can lead to the forgiveness of sins for ourselves and for those for whom we offer the sacrifice.

Removing then from the notion of sacrifice the imperfections associated with it in the past, it is important for Christians to insist that their religion is a sacrificing religion. Sacrifice is that first and most necessary act of religion by which we acknowledge God as our Lord and Father and express our loving dependence on him.

To Belong to One Another

The language of our sacrifice is the language of love. We might understand it better by thinking of two people in love giving each other gifts. The gifts are a sign of their desire to belong to each other, for that is part of what true love really means.

But what does it mean 'to belong to another'? It means making the other person the centre of one's world. It means dethroning oneself and one's selfishness and making the other person the point of reference of one's actions. Clearly this is saying a lot, something too deep for words, and that is why people moved by a deep love will spontaneously reach out for signs and symbols like the giving of gifts to express these inexpressible depths of commitment they experience within themselves.

Now this language for expressing the inexpressible reaches its highest point in sacrifice. Here God is the loved one, and to say that we want to belong to him is not only one of the most fundamental things we can say about our whole manner of life but it also touches off some of the deepest chords within us.

To love God and to belong to him is what existence is all about. He is the source and goal of everything we do and of everything we are. The ultimate reason why we sacrifice is because that is the right order of things. Through sacrifice we express and commit ourselves anew to the truth about what we are. We know that we do not live up to that commitment, and we would like our lives to be more in conformity with that truth than they are. But in the meantime we wish to keep alive in our hearts and before God this basic fact: we belong to him. That is reality. That is our place in the scheme of things. Let us keep that much alive at least, for if we once let this fact slip away from us, we will have handed ourselves over to a great darkness and to a deep delusion.

> *Was not Christ immolated once in himself, and yet he is immolated for the multitudes in the sacrament, not only at the celebration of Easter but even every day?*
>   St Augustine

19   SACRIFICE AND COVENANT

Between God and his people there is a bond that has no equal. On the one hand he has promised his people his special love and providence, and, on the other, they, for their part, have promised to live according to his will. This set of relationships is what we mean by the covenant. Other words for it might be 'union' or 'alliance'. In some ways it is like a marriage. Just as the union between husband and wife is a kind of covenant between them, so the divine covenant has been compared to a marriage between God and his people (for example, Mal 2:14).

The Mosaic Covenant

When the Old Covenant was being established in the revelation made to Moses, we can see very clearly three points in particular which are always important in a covenant. First of all, the covenant began with an act of God. We human beings cannot make a covenant with God on our own. God has to start it all. Divine covenants are acts of divine love and mercy. As Padraig Pearse said in one of his poems, it is not for us 'to bargain or huxter with God.'

After God has made a start, then the people can respond. We see this in the case of the covenant under Moses, when the people accepted the revelation of God's will and undertook to live by it. Covenants are not matters of coercion. They depend on our freedom and on our love.

Thirdly, the covenant was ratified publicly in a solemn liturgical act. Covenants are made by sacrifice, says the Psalmist in Ps 49(50):5, and that is what happened on Sinai. A special sacrifice was celebrated in which the covenant was formally established.

We can read all this in the twenty-fourth chapter of the Book of Exodus. After the immolation of a number of sacrificial victims, Moses formally read out to the Israelites a statement of the law of the covenant, namely the ten commandments. They replied that they would obey all that the Lord required of them. Then Moses took some of the sacrificial blood and sprinkled the people with it, saying, 'This is the blood of the covenant which the Lord has made with you concerning all these words' (Exod 24:8).

The New Covenant

When we turn to the New Testament we find echoes of this saying of Moses in the account of our Lord's words at the Last Supper as we find them in Mark and Matthew. Over the Eucharistic cup our Lord says, 'This is my blood of the covenant, poured out for many' (Mk 14:24). The similarity of these words with those of Moses is no coincidence. It shows us how already in that early community the Eucharist was seen to be part of a sacrificial ritual, a covenant-making ritual. Just as on Sinai the old covenant was established by the sacrifice of Moses, so on Calvary a new covenant was established by the sacrifice of Christ, and this covenant is ratified and renewed for the new people of God in the sacrificial ritual of the Mass.

This then is the new and everlasting covenant which is celebrated and renewed in every Eucharist. The old covenant has come to an end, and our Lord has come among us to establish a whole new set of relationships between heaven and earth. In the Sermon on the Mount he reveals to us his new law, but it is only on Calvary that he gives us that sacrifice which alone makes the living of his covenant possible.

Every Sunday the people of God gather to renew their covenant with the Lord. Sometimes our liturgists can get impatient with the difficulty of creating an atmosphere of worship in our large congregations. They would prefer the warmth and intimacy of a small group at prayer, not to say an elite group at prayer. But the large crowds in our churches are a good reminder of the people gathered at the foot of Sinai or around Christ at the Sermon on the Mount. It is true that our congregations can often be noisy and distracting. There are babies crying and sometimes even dogs running about. But that is just how it was at Sinai and at the Mountain of the Beatitudes, and that is the way it should be – simply the people of God in this place gathered for worship. That is how our Lord likes it, to have them with him, all gathered in from the highways and byways, but still the people of God, renewing their covenant with their Maker.

Renewing the Covenant

We said that it is only the sacrifice of Christ which makes possible the living of the covenant. Our covenant with God is a precarious thing. From the side of God it is unshakeable, but from the side of our humanity it is weak and insecure. We know from our own experience how often we fall away from it when we fail to live up to our Lord's standards of love and service. That is one reason why we are constantly coming back to renew and restore our covenant, our alliance, with God. Any sacrifice of a sinful, wayward humanity has to have this aspect of reparation, of making up lost ground and getting back on to the right track again.

It is above all in the Mass that this is made possible for us. By his death on the cross, in obedience to the Father, Christ, the perfect human being, lived out the new covenant to perfection. In doing this he won for us the grace that would reconcile us to God when we fall away, and would give us the strength to take up our crosses after him. Week after week, then, we come back to Christ in the Mass, to renew the links that bind us to God, and to draw from Christ's sacrifice something of his strength. For this bread, as St. John has it, is the bread of life, 'born-again-life' (Jn 3:3 and 6:54); or, as we find in Matthew, '... for this is my blood of the covenant, which is poured out for many for the forgiveness of sins' (Mt 26:28).

> *This is the sacrifice of Christians – many one body in Christ – this is the practice of the Church in the sacrament of the altar, where it is clear to her that she herself is a victim in the Victim she offers.*
> St Augustine

20   THE GIVER AND THE GIFT

One of the most striking things about the Eucharist is its simplicity. This is not the simplicity of the superficial and the facile, but the simplicity of that which is truly great and truly profound.

We have already seen how our Lord determined the external form of the worship which he left to his community, not taking it from the pomp and splendour of the liturgy of the Temple, but from the familiarity and ordinariness of Jewish daily life. The external form of the Eucharist comes from the simple table rituals of bread and cup and prayer which were part and parcel of the routine life of the Jewish home. Our Lord took these familiar rituals and transformed them. In a Christian context they are now endowed with a profound meaning, being the vehicle of Christ's own act of worship which he gave us at the Last Supper and on the cross. Nevertheless something of the simplicity and ordinariness of their origins still marks their external form.

Christ Giving Himself
However, the simplicity of the Eucharist is shown above all in what Christ is doing here. In the Eucharist Christ gives us himself. It is as simple and as astonishing as that, and yet the heart of the Eucharistic mystery is here. In the sacrament Christ is not giving us just an idea about himself, a visible word clothed in liturgy. Nor is he giving us just a symbol of himself. Indeed he is not even content with working in us the effects of his power and goodness and mercy. He does all these things, but he does more. He gives us himself, his entire self, body, blood, soul and divinity. To each of us he says, 'This is my body, this is my blood.'

Two Truths
In coming to understand the Eucharist a bit more clearly, there are two main truths we have been trying to appreciate. The first is that the Eucharist is the sacrifice of Christ. The second is that the Eucharist is Christ's body and blood. Each of these truths

helps us to understand the other. It is hard to know which comes first, but either would be incomplete without the other.

We have already come to appreciate that the Eucharist is no empty memorial of Calvary: it is the one sacrifice of Christ made actual amongst us. We are now going on to consider this further wonder: our offerings are no longer bread and wine but Christ's very self, body, blood, soul and divinity. Both truths are summed up by saying that the Eucharist is Christ giving himself.

First of all, it really is Christ giving *himself*. That is to say that it is his very self that he gives us, body, blood, soul and divinity. But then this comes about by Christ *giving* himself. Christ giving himself is really what Calvary was. On the cross Christ gave himself to the Father and he gave himself to us: it was in giving himself to the Father that he gave himself to us; and it was in giving himself to us that he gave himself to the Father – two aspects of the one action. We might sum it up by saying that in the sacrifice Christ shows that he is giving himself to the Father, and in holy communion he shows that he is giving himself to us.

This giving of himself is the action in which Calvary becomes present in the Mass. Christ lays down on our altars his body and his blood just as truly as he laid them down on the altar of the cross. It is the same action of the same love, now carried out ritually, just as once it was carried out historically.

Where God Is To Be Found

Once we see how communion and sacrifice belong together, in the way in which it has just been presented, we will appreciate more clearly what is happening when Christ in the sacrament gives us nothing less than his own body and blood. In giving us these he is giving us his sacrifice. He is drawing us more deeply into the movement of his worship, enabling us to live off his sacrifice and nourishing us with that self-giving which was central to the cross. As St Paul tells us in the tenth chapter of First Corinthians, union with Christ in the Eucharist is a sharing in the victim of a sacrifice. The Eucharist is saying to us that God is found here below, not in self-seeking, but in self-surrender. If we want to live the truth of this ritual, our worship must be for us an ever deeper dedication to giving ourselves more completely to God and to others in our daily lives.

The Offering of Ourselves
Our self-giving must be real because Christ's was so real. On the cross he really gave himself to the last drop of his blood. Nothing less would do. When this same action is recaptured ritually in the Eucharist, the reality of his self-giving is brought home to us by the change of our offerings into his body and blood. Nothing less would do. But it will all be in vain unless we go out from Mass to live lives of dedication to God and to others. That is what it means to be a Christian. Nothing less will do.

> The cup of blessing which we bless, is it not communion with the blood of Christ? The bread that we break, is it not communion with the body of Christ?
> (1 Cor 10:16)

21   THE BREAD OF GOD

Some years ago our cinemas showed a documentary on a theme so ordinary that you would wonder why they would make a film of it – bread. Yes, our daily bread! But bread can be a beautiful and variegated thing. It comes in so many different shapes and textures; and then it is such a familiar and necessary part of human life. Our daily bread has the familiarity of a friend. Indeed it is a symbol of our daily task. We call it 'the staff of life.'

A Most Important Use

That documentary, however, failed to mention one of the most important and universal of the uses which people have found for bread. Being an obvious sign of human life, bread is very commonly used by religious people as a sign of their worship. Through the symbolism of bread people feel that they can bring their entire existence with them into the presence of God and so offer it to their Maker.

In trying to understand a bit more the gifts we bring to the Mass and what happens them there, we might begin with bread, seeing it as not just a physical substance with certain chemical properties. These have no great importance in the Mass, once it is established that our hosts are indeed what people mean by bread, namely a food made from wheat. It is bread in its human and religious meaning that is really important in the Mass. The great change that takes place there does not affect the chemical properties of our offerings. It is through a change in the meaning of our offerings that Christ's body and blood are made present on our altars.

The Meaning of the Gifts

What, then, one might ask, is the human and religious meaning of our gifts? At the beginning of the Mass we might see them as simply signs of our personal worship. We, the local community, gather together and wish to place our entire existence as human beings and as Christians into the hands of God. For us Christians, as for so many other religious people in the world, bread and wine are ready-made signs of that existence, as we saw in a previous chapter.

Bread, 'our daily bread,' is especially the sign of our labour
and of our struggle to make ends meet. Wine, the noblest
drink we have, is especially a sign of joy and of all that is
noblest in life. It is the whole of life, then, in all its joys and
sorrows, which we place on the paten and in the cup of the
Mass.

But who are we to think that we can give gifts to God? Can
we really bridge the gap between heaven and earth and make
offerings that are really pleasing to the Father? As long as our
offerings express nothing more than what we ourselves are,
then they are of no avail. Indeed, as long as we are simply a
local gathering on our own, trying to reach up to heaven by
dint of our own imagination and will-power, we are no better
than the people in the book of Genesis building the tower of
Babel (Gen 11:1-9), and our worship is in vain.

To be more accurate, that is the way things would be, if
Christ had not come to the rescue. Of course he has come, and
that makes all the difference. He has taken over our worship, for
he is the only one who can bridge the gap between heaven and
earth. He is the only one who can offer to the Father a worship
that is truly pleasing in his sight. Consequently, he has come to
change our worship into his own, and this change affects
everything about the Mass – its meaning, its offerer, its gifts.

Our Worship Transformed

He changes the meaning of what we do. To outward
appearances we are just a local gathering which has come
together to worship God in word and sign, in bread and wine
and prayer. But Christ has changed the inner reality of what we
do. In saying over our bread and wine, 'This is my body, this is
my blood,' our Lord is equivalently saying, 'This is my
worship.' He is changing our worship into his own. He is
identifying what we do with what he did on the cross when he

offered to his Father the greatest act of love and worship in the whole history of human worship.

He changes the offerer. To the casual observer the offerer of Sunday worship is just the local congregation of believers. But in the teaching of the Church the local congregation is a sign of the whole body of Christ, head and members, which is made present in this place by its local members when they gather with their priest at the altar. The true offerer of the Mass therefore is not just the local assembly but the whole body of Christ, head and members, in heaven and earth and under the earth, gathered around Christ our High Priest, in whose person the ordained priest celebrates.

Christ changes our gifts. At the beginning of our worship they are but bread and wine, signs of our existence which we wish to give to God. By the central action of Christ in the Mass, our worship is changed into the great mystery of worship which Christ himself offered on Calvary. But this same action requires that our offerings be changed into that which he offered on the cross, his own body and blood. As long as the offerings stand simply for our worship, it is enough if they remain simply bread and wine. But they cannot truly mean Christ's worship on the cross unless they become what he offered there, his own body and blood. Their new meaning requires the new reality.

Communion in the Sacrifice

Perhaps this fact will help to underline another truth about the Mass to which we keep coming back in this book. The Eucharist is sacrificial through and through. The sacrifice is not just a way of bringing about the Real Presence. The Real Presence itself is sacrificial in that it is the presence of Christ in his self-giving. The change in our offerings comes about because the sacrifice of Christ requires it. Too often we have made a divide between sacrifice and communion, between Mass and tabernacle.

In the Old Testament, bread that had been offered in sacrifice was called the bread of God. We might learn from St Ignatius of Antioch (d. circa 110 AD) who applied this expression to the Eucharist. Every consecrated host is the bread of God by being the sign of Christ's sacrifice on the cross, and there is no true devotion to holy communion without our entering into the movement of Christ's self-offering. In the canon of the Mass we carry out in our hearts what in holy communion we carry out in flesh and blood, namely our identifying ourselves with Christ in his self-gift for the life of the world.

The Sacrament for Children

There is one special difficulty with regard to the doctrine in this chapter which might be mentioned before we conclude. Any teacher of small children, especially those preparing them for the sacrament for the first time, might well wonder how to lead their small charges into these truths. Well, it must be admitted that entry into the mysteries of the Eucharist is a gradual process in life. Young children can scarcely appreciate the kind of truths being considered here. For them the first thing is to grasp that the host is no longer bread but Christ himself. In this way they will learn the importance of growing in the love of our Lord and of welcoming his presence in a special sense in the sacrament. Without getting involved in the language of 'body' and 'blood', their minds can focus on the teaching that Christ is whole and entire in each host, and receiving the sacrament is a special way simply of receiving the person of Christ into their hearts.

> *The Eucharist is the flesh of our Saviour Jesus Christ, who suffered for our sins, which the Father raised by his goodness.*
> St Ignatius of Antioch

22   THE BREAD OF LIFE

Holy communion is all about change. The Eucharist is Christ changing the world. He changes us; he changes our worship and he changes our gifts. At the beginning of Mass, as has been explained in a previous chapter, our gifts are simply bread and wine, the signs of our ordinary life which we wish to give to God. By the time of the communion of the Mass these gifts have become Christ's body and blood, and all this as part of God's design that through these gifts we be changed, so that we in turn might help him in the changing of the world.

The Divine Activity

Truly the action of God is wonderful! It is not confined simply to the world of ideas. The divine action overflows heaven and is at work here below. It can change the course of real events, if providence so requires it. It can change us too, from within, changing not simply our ideas but our hearts, our habits and our inmost selves.

Surely this throws a little light on the mystery of holy communion. In the Eucharist, through his Holy Spirit, Christ changes bread and wine into his own body and blood, because part of his purpose is to change us. This same deep-reaching action of the Spirit of God, which changes our gifts, is going to change our hearts, which the gifts represent.

But, some will say, we do not see any change. In the Eucharist the external appearances of our offerings remain the same shape, colour and taste. That is true, and that is necessary if the gifts are to remain signs for our faith, so that we may continue to come to the Eucharistic Christ under the signs of offering and nourishment. But while the outer appearances remain the same, faith knows that the inner reality has been changed. This is what we mean by transubstantiation.

The Change in Ourselves

Similarly with the change in ourselves. On going to holy communion we cannot always claim that we feel differently. Maybe it does happen sometimes, and then it is a consolation that we should welcome, as long as we do not depend on it. A change may or may not take place in our feelings, but the inner change is the one our Lord is most concerned about, and that is something which goes to the very depths of our being. This is a change which reaches beneath the surface of moods and feelings. It touches the secret mainsprings of our actions and helps us to keep on developing in the slow, sure process of growing up into the fullness of Christ.

The Need for Faith

Just as we need faith to accept the change of bread and wine, so we need faith to accept the reality of this inner change in grace. But this is the way the Christian tradition, East and West, has always spoken. It begins with St Paul, where we read that we are being renewed from day to day (2 Cor 4:16) and that we are being changed into the likeness of Christ (2 Cor 3:18). The great saints of the Eastern Church would tell us that we are being transformed, transfigured, divinized by the growing reality of God's presence within us. In the West, saints like St Augustine and St Leo would say that, as bread becomes the Eucharistic body of Christ, so the Church nourished by this sacrament becomes more fully the mystical body of Christ. But always we are being changed by a new life within us, and that life is nourished, strengthened and maintained by the food and drink of the sacrament.

More Than Human

If the Christian life were simply a matter of being human and doing good, then it would fit in with that view that the elements of Christian worship should be nothing more than the bread and wine of ordinary usage, made holy indeed by the context of worship, but in themselves nothing more than bread and wine. Perhaps it is only when we begin to see the Eucharist within the Christian mystery as a whole, and the extraordinary lengths to which Divine Love has gone for his people generally, that we can come to see how fitting it is that this same divine generosity should do such extraordinary things for us in the sacrament.

The Whole Christian Mystery

It is true that Christian life involves being human and doing good, but it achieves such ends only by being so much more than that. Christian life is nothing less than the divine life. Scripture tells us that it means being sharers of the divine nature (2 Pet 1:4). It means living by the life of God himself, sharing something of his strength and so coming to take on the image of one of the divine Persons, Jesus Christ our Lord. Those who eat this flesh and drink this blood have eternal life (Jn 6:54), that is to say, they already have something of the life of God himself within them.

It is when we see that this is the ultimate purpose of the sacrament in the plan of Christ that we can come to appreciate a little more why our gifts are no longer bread and wine. Bread and wine will do for sustaining ordinary human life. But to sustain the divine life, the life of God himself, this is something which only God himself can do; and so Christ does it by giving us himself. He signalled the fact on the stage of human history by laying down his body and blood on the cross. He achieves the purpose of Calvary and the purpose of the Eucharist when he feeds us with his body and blood in the Mass

> *You have been taught and fully instructed that what seems to be bread is not bread, though it appears to be such to the taste, but the body of Christ; that what seems to be wine is not wine, though the taste would have it so, but the blood of Christ.*
> St Cyril of Jerusalem (d. 386 AD)

23 TRANSFIGURATION

Of the many remarkable events recounted in the Gospels, few are as striking as the story of Christ's transfiguration. For just one blinding moment something of the inner reality of Christ, hidden throughout many humdrum years, suddenly shines out before his three disciples. For that brief instant they get some idea of the mystery present in Christ all along but ordinarily veiled from their sight. As St Ephraem (d. 373 AD) put it: just as his clothing covered the weakness of his body, so his body veiled the splendour of his divinity. But on the mountain of the transfiguration it was different. Here his divinity shone through his body and his face dazzled them like the sun (Mt 17:2).

Future Glory

In one place in scripture we are told that in heaven something like that is going to happen to all the friends of Christ. 'Then shall the just shine as the sun in the kingdom of their Father' (Mt 13:43). We are familiar with how this has already come about for our Lady in the mystery of her Assumption. But one day it is to happen to all of us, if we keep true to Christ.

The body which Christ took from his mother was as human and as ordinary as that of any of us, but through contact with the inner mystery of Christ it came under those far from ordinary influences which go with the power and mission of the God-man. When the Word was made flesh, it was not just a wonder for a day and then was all over. It was rather the beginning of a process. The Word's being made flesh was part of a great plan by which all flesh, all human kind, is to be lifted up into the divine presence. We are to be transformed into a state of being which the human heart has never even dreamed of (1 Cor 2:9).

In the New Testament a similar word is used for this process as is used for that which happened to Christ on Mt Tabor. We will all be *transfigured*. 'Heaven is where we belong, and from there we are expecting a Saviour, the Lord Jesus Christ, who will transfigure these bodies of our lowliness to be like his glorious body, according to the power by which he can subdue all things to himself' (Phil 3:20f). Tabor was not only a revelation of what Christ already was. It also gave us a glimpse of something we ourselves, in a lesser way, are to become.

A New Earth

Indeed it is not only the followers of Christ that this mystery touches. There are hints in the New Testament that it is going to envelop the whole of creation. On the Last Day there will be a new heaven and a new earth (Apoc 21:1). The whole of creation will be set free (Rom 8:20). The cosmic Christ, the centre of the universe, will be all in all (Col 3:11), and he will celebrate a truly cosmic liturgy when he hands over all things into the hands of his Father, so that God may be all in all (1 Cor 15:28).

These are mysterious truths. We speak of things which eye has not seen nor ear heard. Yet it is good sometimes to raise our heads above the drabness of our ordinary existence and to look forward to the splendours of that vision which our faith holds for us in the future.

Christ Changing the World

But the future is prepared for in the present, and there is a sense in which the transfiguration of the universe is already under way. The fact is that, in making his love a reality among us, Christ is changing the world. By communicating his divine life to his friends he is transfiguring the human race. We see this most clearly in the lives of the saints, but it is already a fact in all who are living the life of grace. Christ is helping us to grow in love, and love transfigures those whom it touches.

The Eucharist as Centre

At the centre of the transfiguration of the world stands the Eucharist. Indeed, some of the early saints refer to transubstantiation as the *transfiguration* of our bread and wine. How else will that preparation for a new heaven and earth be carried on if not by the sacrament of the altar? It is above all from his place at the centre of the Eucharist that Christ is working for the transfiguration of the universe.

One day Christ will transfigure our bodies in the resurrection from the dead. Indeed by this same power he will subdue and transfigure the entire universe. Now it is by this same power, at work in the sacrament, that he changes bread and wine into his own body and blood. The transfiguration of the universe began on the morning of the resurrection, when Christ's body rose from the dead. It is continued in every Mass as bread and wine are changed into his glorified body and precious blood. Our humble gifts are touched by something of that final mystery and conflagration; they are consumed by the closeness of God; and as his divinity shone through his body on Tabor and glorified it on the morning of the resurrection, so we know that it is present at the heart of every host and has changed it into the flesh and blood of the Son of God.

Jesus Is God

In the tradition of the Church the mystery of Tabor has always helped to bring people back to one of the central truths about Christ: Jesus is God. In the long run you cannot explain Jesus of Nazareth and all he has done in the world without eventually coming to the divinity at the centre of his person. If our notion of Christ could get by without invoking his divinity, then we well might wonder whether we are really talking about Jesus at all!

This is especially true of the Eucharist. Church tradition has always taught extraordinary things about this sacrament; but if it can make such claims, it is only because Christians have believed that at the centre of the Eucharist is the divinity of Christ. This sacrament is extraordinary because divinity is at the heart of it. Any human being with a sense of drama can give us bread and wine as tokens of his body and blood, but only a divine person can change bread and wine into his very self. The mystery of transfiguration in the Eucharist brings us back ultimately to the same fact as the mystery of transfiguration on Mt Tabor. This is the Son of God. Lord, it is good for us to be here.

> *As it is written: eye has not seen, nor ear heard, nor has it entered into the human heart to conceive the things God has prepared for those that love him.*
> (1 Cor 2:9)

24   EUCHARIST AND COMMUNITY

So far in this book attention has been on the question: What is the Eucharist? We have traced the sacrament back to its origins and seen in what sense it is sacrifice and banquet and mystery of presence. Having thrown some light on these aspects of our subject, it is now time to turn to another fundamental question: what does the Eucharist do? To put it bluntly, what is it for? Does it make any difference in our world? In what sense, if any, is it close to the concerns that move people in our world today?

This is a question about the effects or fruits of the Eucharist, and in this book they will be summed up under three headings, which are going to be explained in this and in the next three chapters. At the Last Supper our Lord told the disciples that they are to go out and bear fruit, fruit that will last (Jn 15:16). We can apply this general command of his to the fruits of the Eucharist in particular.

Sacrament of Love

The first fruit of the Eucharist and the basis of all the other fruits follows immediately from what the Eucharist itself is. We have seen that this sacrament is the masterpiece of God's love, his way of extending into the lives of each of us that love of which Christ gave the uttermost proof in his self-sacrifice on the cross (Jn 15:13). Love, therefore, is the key to the Eucharist. The concern which was clearly uppermost in our Lord's mind in John's account of the Last Supper was that we should love one another (Jn 13:34f; 15:12, 17; 17:21). This then is the same concern which he has in the Eucharist, and so the first fruit of the sacrament has to be our union in love of one another around the one table with Christ.

It is a matter of two loves in one. The basis of it all has to be that love for God which we learn from Jesus in his self-surrender to the Father, made present in the sacrifice. But the love of God cannot be confined. Of its nature it overflows into the love of our fellow human beings, since Christ died not just for you and for me but for every living person who ever walked this earth. This is the unforgettable teaching of the great letter of the apostle John, which reads like a commentary on his account of the Last Supper.

In this we have come to know love, that he laid down his life for us, and we ought to lay down our lives for our brothers ... If God so loved us, we ought to love one another ... If anyone says, 'I love God' and hates his brother, he is a liar, for he who does not love his brother, whom he sees, cannot love the God he does not see (1 Jn 3:16; 4:11, 20).

The New Sense of Community

When the Second Vatican Council came to talk about the Eucharist, the principal aspect of the sacrament which it wished to treat was its effect on human community. This was in line with the general teaching of the council that our faith is not just 'pie in the sky' but should make a difference already in this life (*Gaudium et spes*, art. 40). When older people today compare the Mass with the way it was before the reforms of Vatican II, they will often say how much they miss the sense of mystery which was so much a part of the Mass in their younger days. While one hopes that a sense of mystery will not be lost completely, it is true that this aspect has been scaled down in the new liturgy. This could be a matter of considerable regret until one realizes the importance of the value which the Church wants to put in its place. There is always a danger that our religion become over-individualistic, each of us concerned only about our own private salvation. The council wished to change all that and so to make the sense of community central to our liturgy.

> No Christian community, however, is built up unless it is rooted and centred in the celebration of the most holy Eucharist. This is where all education in the spirit of community must begin
> (*The Ministry and Life of Priests,* art. 6)

The First Community

The first human community is the family. The council referred to it as the 'domestic church' (*Lumen gentium*, art. 11). It is the place where Christian love bears its most immediate and far-reaching fruit. If one can say that 'the family that prays together stays together,' then this must be true with special force of the family that comes together around the sacrifice of Christ and is nourished by him at the one table.

The Local Community

When the faithful have been rooted and grounded in God's love through a sound Christian upbringing, the influence of their Eucharistic life will spread outward in ever-widening circles.

Genuine worship at Mass must inevitably bear fruit in the way
we live our lives from Mass to Mass, in the work-place and our
places of leisure, enabling us to build up the life of the local
community and to come to the aid of those in need.

Society at Large

But the circles are called to spread further still. One of the most
difficult bridges for human beings to cross is that between living
community on an individual level and living it in the world at
large. Human beings have been referred to as social animals.
We are compelled to relate to one another for the sake of
personal survival, but the kind of community which society in
general stands in need of requires a degree of openness,
commitment, realism and inspiration which most of us sadly
lack. As one writer put it:

> It is clearly no longer enough to be social animals, babbling
> together at cocktail parties, and brawling with each other
> in business and over boundaries. It is our task – our critical,
> essential, crucial task – to transform ourselves from mere
> social creatures into community creatures. It is the only
> way that human evolution will be able to proceed.[5]

What could possibly be the agent of such a transformation? In
terms of secular life there is no clear candidate, but the believer
will inevitably think that the Eucharist must have a role to play,
especially in the light of the teaching we have found in Vatican II.

The Church at Large

There is one further circle to be drawn into the picture. If we
accept the teaching already referred to in *Gaudium et spes* art. 40,
then we will be convinced that building human community

---

5. M. Scott Peck *The Different Drum: Community Making and Peace*,
    London: Rider, 1988, p.165

here below is but an aspect of building up the kingdom of God and building up the Church. In this same article the council remarks that the earthly city and the heavenly city penetrate each other. The ultimate effect of the love which the Eucharist feeds and promotes is the building up and extension of the Church of God itself. 'The Eucharist makes the Church,' is the common way of saying that today.

This memorable phrase brings before us the deepest reaches of the social impact of the sacrament. It is not just a question of tapping natural energies or unleashing pent-up human resources. It is not the case that the Eucharist is to be a tool for social engineering. Rather the truth of the matter is that our endeavour for human community at all levels is but part of a larger project which is that of Christ himself in building up his body in this world; and so the forces that go into this project are sustained and enlivened by the mysterious energies that circulate from the head of this body to the members. To put it in a nutshell: the body of Christ makes the body of Christ – the sacramental body makes and builds up the body that is the Church – and this in turn inevitably overflows into human community generally.

> *By the one body which is his own, he blesses through a mysterious participation those who believe in him, and makes them one body with himself and with each other.*
> St Cyril of Alexandria (d. 444)

25   GOD'S LOVE IN ACTION

A friend of mine once met Mother Teresa of Calcutta and asked her to write something in his prayer-book. What she wrote was: 'Be only all for Jesus. Love only Jesus. Give only Jesus to all you meet.' When you think about it, you can see

Mother Teresa's service of the poor as a silent way of giving them Jesus. Actions speak louder than words, we say, and an ancient prayer of our liturgy says, 'Imitate what you celebrate.' In a way what she was doing was imitating the Eucharist, giving Christ to those in need.

Like the prophets of Israel our Lord often conveyed his meaning by actions as much as by words. Breaking the bread at the multiplication of the loaves, he was pointing to his own life as one shared with the poorest of the poor. Washing the disciples' feet at the Last Supper, he was underlining that humble service is the key to authority in his kingdom. Breaking bread and sharing it with us in the Eucharist, he is telling us that the bread is not only himself but our lives also, which in imitation of him should be spent in the sacrificial service of our fellow human beings.

What Do I Get Out Of It?
It is clear from all that has been said so far that Mass is not only about how we relate to God but about how we relate to other people. Unfortunately that is not always the first thought in people's minds as they adore or celebrate this sacrament today. An extreme individualism is one of the heresies of the hour, and Frank Sinatra surely spoke for a whole generation when he sang, 'I do it my way.' Nothing could be further removed from the true spirit of faith and of the Eucharist than such individualism.

One of the most frequent remarks of young people today about the Mass is that it is so boring. As was noted on a previous page, if the priest is lazy or casual about organizing or celebrating the Eucharist, the remark may have a point! But often too one might see behind this remark something of the individualism of which we speak. The mind-set behind the remark can so easily be: What do I get out of it?

What Can I Do For Others?

Very different was the way of thinking which we find in the ancient Church. There they thought as spontaneously in terms of the community as we do in terms of the individual. One ancient writer in third century Syria wrote as follows: 'No one should stay away from the (Sunday) assembly. If they do, they deprive the body of Christ of a member.' In other words, the key question is not, 'What can the Mass do for me?' but rather, 'What can I do for others – through going to Mass, praying for them, offering my life to God on their behalf and re-committing myself through the power of holy communion to a way of life that puts other people first?'

As we have just suggested, the same problem comes up with regard to holy communion. A public controversy in Ireland some time ago about sharing communion with other Churches was another pointer to the way individualism still survives in our thinking about the sacraments. In the nineteenth century piety was often clearly individualistic, a piety that might be described as one of 'me and my Jesus.' The Church was seen as just the necessary provider of the sacraments and not as central to their inner meaning. The recent controversy has shown how many still think of the Eucharist as just a matter between themselves and God, as though the Church has little to do with its inner meaning!

Receiving the Divine Guest

In the liturgy itself two different ways are suggested for thinking about holy communion. The first makes room for the individual in an acceptable way. Each of us at the table of the sacrament comes as an individual to receive the Divine Guest 'under our roof' much as the centurion in the Gospel from whom that phrase has come.[6] In a mysterious way we receive the Divine

---

6.   Lk 7:6. The phrase 'under my roof' has been dropped from the people's response in English, 'Lord I am not worthy to receive you,' but it still appears in the Latin and in other languages such as the Irish.

Guest like Martha and Mary (Lk 10:38) or like the reformed Zacchaeus (Lk 19:6). In his most recent encyclical on the Eucharist (2003), John Paul II remarked of holy communion that each of us receives Christ and Christ receives each of us.

Receiving the Life of the Body

But the sacrament points not only to Christ's body of flesh received by us as individuals, but also to the mysterious body, his Church, of which we are members. This is an aspect of the sacrament which we find expressed, for instance, in the Third Eucharistic Prayer, when we ask to become 'one body, one spirit in Christ.' As St Paul underlines, any man will want to nourish his body and look after it (Eph 5:20). This suggests that holy communion is Christ coming to the members of his body to nourish them with the life that flows from him. What matters here is not what we are to get out of it, but what Christ, as head of the body, wants to achieve through us.

God's Love in Action

Mother Teresa once summed up her vocation as that of being God's love in action for the poorest of the poor. Christ has his plan to reach out to the world through us. In a real sense, as members of his body, we are the extension of Christ into today's world. Through us he still goes around, helping, consoling, and strengthening his people. Through the Eucharist we receive that life by which we are to be Christ's love in action for those around us, making his love a reality in our homes, our places of work, our parish and our world. This is the way Mother Teresa's great namesake, St Teresa of Avila (d. 1582), put it in our concluding quotation.

> *Christ has no body now but yours –*
> *no hands, no feet on earth but yours.*

Yours are the only eyes with which his compassion
can still look out on a troubled world;
Yours are the only feet with which he can go about doing good;
Yours are the only hands with which he can bring his blessing
to his people;
Christ has no body now on earth but yours.
            St Teresa of Avila

26   FORGIVENESS

One aspect of the Mass which is becoming clearer to people as
a result of the new liturgy is the fact that it helps towards the
forgiveness of our sins. This is brought home to us very forcibly
at the beginning of Mass by the act of penance. But it does not
end there. Just as the 'Gloria' of the Mass does not exhaust the
offering of Eucharistic praise, neither does this initial act of
penance exhaust the work of forgiveness and reconciliation in
the Mass.

Atonement
Indeed, this notion of forgiveness is central to what we mean
by saying that the Eucharist is a sacrifice of atonement. An
atoning sacrifice is one that leads to forgiveness of sin. The
Epistle to the Hebrews applied this notion to our Lord's
offering of his body and blood on the cross. In so far as in the
Mass we have that same offering of Calvary made present in a
ritual way, the Church has always believed that Mass is to be
offered for the sins of the living and the dead. As long ago as the
fourth century St Cyril of Jerusalem said of the Mass, 'We offer
Christ slain for our sins, propitiating the loving God both for
the dead and for ourselves.'

Food for the Weak

The Eucharistic sacrifice reaches its consummation in holy communion. The sacrificial banquet sets its seal on our whole act of worship, and this applies no less to the aspect of forgiveness than to all the other fruits of the Eucharist. Perhaps we have not thought enough about holy communion as setting its seal on our forgiveness and reconciliation. Sometimes in the past there has been a tendency to regard holy communion as in some way a reward for virtue rather than as the strengthening and consolation of the weak. To keep holy communion for an exceptional elite is Jansenism, and it goes against the whole development of frequent communion in the modern Church. We should take to heart the fact that the Eucharist is food, and food is for the weak as well as for the strong.

That the Eucharist gives the forgiveness of sins is a truth already present in the New Testament. In St Matthew's version of the Last Supper, our Lord says of the Eucharistic cup that it is his blood 'for the forgiveness of sins' (Mt 26:28). Many of the great Eucharistic Prayers of the Eastern Church have made a special point of this forgiveness communicated in the Eucharist. In our western liturgy it is above all in the post-communion prayers that this same intention comes to the fore.

Confession before Communion

Of course we must keep in mind the ordinary law of the Church by which sacramental absolution is required before a person who has been in grave sin may go to holy communion. On the other hand, the fact remains that the tradition of the Church has always looked to holy communion as itself one of the special channels of the forgiveness of sin for Christians. That being so, you will be wondering where this teaching leaves the sacrament of Penance. It is clear enough that Penance will have a role in the cases of grave sin, but the place of confessions of devotion might seem far from clear, namely the place of confessions where only venial sins need to be confessed.

The growing appreciation of the gift of forgiveness in the Mass will certainly make a difference to our ordinary confessions of devotion. This is one of the factors that contributes in some cases to a reduction in the number of confessions. Nevertheless, far from making this sacrament superfluous, these developments can, if anything, deepen our approach to sacramental reconciliation.

In the past we tended to regard confession as simply the sacrament of forgiveness. As we come to appreciate how forgiveness can come to us in other ways besides confession, then we are more likely to see how there is more to confession than just telling our sins and getting absolution for them. Confession is the sacrament of penance precisely. As long as there is penance in our lives, there will be a place for confession, even for confessions of devotion, for we will always have need to bring our penitential efforts under the strengthening hand of Christ in this sacrament. In confessions of devotion there is forgiveness for our venial sins, just as there is in the Eucharist, but in a different way and with a different spirit.

Eucharist and Penance
One modern writer, Karl Rahner, has put it well, writing of the Eucharist as follows: 'The primary and proper purpose of the Eucharist cannot be sinful man's appearance before the tribunal of divine grace, and therefore a man cannot, when receiving the Eucharist, really elicit the acts of a sinner before that tribunal of God.'[7] That is the proper purpose and spirit of the sacrament of Penance.

---

7.   *Servants of the Lord*, London, 1968, p. 179.

The sacrament of Penance is where we face up to the truth about ourselves and to all the dark and negative things in our living of the Christian life. The Eucharist, on the other hand, is the most positive Christian act. The moment of communion in particular is one of joy and celebration for the wonders of God's love and mercy. If it includes forgiveness amongst its gifts, it does so just as an aspect of something larger, somewhat after the manner of that feast which greeted the prodigal son when he returned to the father's house: for he who was dead has come to life again, and he who was lost is found.

This is a most consoling truth. One of the most important things about it is the way it helps to make possible the practice of frequent, and even daily communion. It underlines that the faults and failings of every day are never a reason for staying away from the Eucharist. Indeed they should only strengthen our resolve to come to the table of reconciliation and to take our place with Christ, as the sinners did in the Gospel (Mt 9:10-13). St Ambrose once referred to communion as our daily bread for our daily sins. If, as the saying goes, even the just person falls seven times a day, then we all have all the more need of these continuous cleansing graces, which are always being offered to us at the Saviour's welcoming table.

> As we eat his flesh which he gave for us, we grow in strength, and as we drink his blood which he poured out for us, we are washed clean.
>
> Preface I of the Holy Eucharist

27   THE GREAT BANQUET

In one place in the Acts of the Apostles we are given an unforgettable image of that time which our Lord spent with his disciples after the resurrection: We are those, says St Peter, 'who ate and drank with him after he rose from the dead' (Acts

10:41). Indeed it is remarkable how often in those resurrection appearances of our Lord there is mention of the disciples eating and drinking with Christ.

The Messianic Banquet

In fact these occasions were more than just meals together. They were signs, pointers, telling people of a greater reality which lies in the future, but which these meals were felt to anticipate. Sometimes in the New Testament heaven is presented to us under the image of a meal. The Jews often thought of the final triumph of the Messiah as being like a great banquet, at which the Messiah would come and sit down to table with his friends

Pledge of Future Glory

In the tradition of the Church this future Messianic Banquet is anticipated here below, not only in those resurrection scenes we have mentioned, but in every Eucharist. This is the sense in which the Eucharist is called in scripture 'the Lord's Supper', or 'the Supper of the Lamb'. 'Happy are those who are called to his Supper' echoes the Angel of the Apocalypse before the Messianic Banquet (Apoc 19:9). Rightly we anticipate his invitation at the communion of every Mass.

The Eucharist is not a meal in the physical sense of the term. A little wafer and a sip from a cup are not, in any ordinary human sense of the term, a meal. A meal implies a certain fullness, and that is clearly not present in the Eucharist in any external sense.

Sign of His Coming

Externally, the Eucharist is a ritual; that is to say, it is a sign. We have already seen how it is a sign of that great event in which the whole history of the Church was born, namely in the sacrifice of the cross. But we are now seeing that it is also a sign of another great event, namely of the coming of Christ at the end of time – in that great Messianic Banquet, when we are all to sit down with Abraham, Isaac and Jacob in the kingdom of the Father (Mt 8:11). But this sign is of a special kind. It is a sacramental sign. Now the mark of a sacramental sign is that it contains that which it signifies. The Eucharistic ritual, therefore, contains the sacrifice of the cross, and so it is really, though sacramentally, a sacrifice. In a similar way this same ritual contains Christ's Messianic Banquet, and so it is really, though sacramentally, a banquet.

Banquet means fullness, but what is the fullness which belongs to the Lord's Supper and is anticipated in the Eucharist? It is the divine life. It is communion with God himself, Father, Son and Holy Spirit. In the Eucharist we are given an anticipation of that communion with God which is to be our happiness in heaven for ever: 'Anyone who eats my flesh and drinks my blood has eternal life' (Jn 6:54).

Communion
A true meal is an act of communion. It is a group of people sharing together. In this way it is one of our best images of what divine life means. Often we think of divine life, the life of grace, as some mysterious material substance imparted to us by the sacraments. There is a certain truth behind that image, and the image itself is suggested by the New Testament. Christ, we are told, is the vine and we are the branches. It is easy then to compare our union with him to the sap circulating in the vine.

Personal Union
At the same time such an image can miss the main point about our union with God. This union is principally a personal one,

based on knowing and loving God. It is a living and loving communion with Father, Son and Holy Spirit. One day this communion is to hold our minds and hearts in the unspeakable happiness of eternity. Here below it comes to us already, dimly perhaps, known only to faith, but really known and really possessed, a mystery growing within us. The Eucharist strengthens and deepens within us that life by which already here below we can know and love Father, Son and Holy Spirit in preparation for the joys of eternity.

The Eucharist then must be one of the moments in our lives for an explicit and heartfelt turning to God. In every communion Father Son and Holy Spirit give themselves to each of us in an ever-deepening way. Surely we are a heartless and thankless people if we do not respond to their goodness with deep and appreciative personal prayer. As was pointed out in chapter 12 above, if we cannot do this adequately in the course of the Mass itself, we should think nothing of staying behind after Mass for special moments of such personal prayer. They are among the most precious moments God gives us here below. This is also a point of special importance when forming young children for holy communion: we must teach them from the beginning how to pray after holy communion and so to discover God in a personal way.

Unsearchable Riches
It was St Ambrose who first referred to the Eucharist as 'this divine sacrament', and when one considers the teaching which has just been given, one can see that this description is no exaggeration. One cannot but be aware how sharply this view contrasts with a more humanistic way of thinking about liturgy which is sometimes put forward today out of a desire to build a bridge between our liturgy and the spirit of the times. Unfortunately, however, this humanistic kind of approach very

easily reduces the Eucharist to a celebration of human togetherness and little more, which is surely greatly to underestimate the 'unsearchable riches' which the Lord, in his goodness, has hidden in his sacraments. The Mass is not simply an act of human fellowship, and holy communion is not just some kind of holy party.

It is true that in the Eucharist we rejoice in brotherhood and sisterhood with one another, but this sacrament expresses what the whole of Christian history teaches us, namely that true human fellowship is impossible for us unless it be discovered in the gift of God. It is only when we open ourselves to God and let him raise us above ourselves in grace that we can come to a love that is in anyway lasting and truly Christian.

This is why any playing down of the divine mystery of the Eucharist in the name of some facile 'relevance' and superficial 'togetherness' is not only false to what God has revealed about the sacrament, but also undermines in advance that genuine human community which the Eucharist is meant to inspire and to deepen. If we are to love, let us first learn what the word means at the table of the divine Trinity and at the foot of the cross in the Mass. Let us first steep ourselves in the mystery of communion in the sacrament, so that, when we go out from Mass, we can bring to those around us a love that is more than human and something more than ourselves.

> *The absolute generosity, which the Trinity simply is, remains the universally dominant background of the mystery of saving worship in Christ.*
> E. Schillebeeckx[8]

---

8. *Christ the Sacrament of the Encounter with God*, London 1963, p. 46.

PART III

LIVING THE EUCHARIST

28 THE EUCHARIST IN CHRISTIAN LIFE

In this, the third part of this book, the subject continues to be the Eucharist, but in this section our basic question will concern not just what the sacrament means in itself, but what it means *for us* and for a Eucharistic way of life. Now you cannot reflect on the Eucharist in that way without reflecting on Christian life more generally, for the Eucharist is the celebration and manifestation of what Christian life really is.

What is Christian life anyway? To put it another way, what does it mean to be a Christian? Most of us would probably give different answers to that question. It is something I have been asking myself recently, looking back over experiences when somebody did something for me and I said, 'That was a truly Christian thing to do!' When people are really loving and unselfish towards others, that is what we mean by Christianity in action. The idea is not very original, but that does not prevent you appreciating the reality when you meet it and you are in need.

The Two Movements of Love

To love and be unselfish like that requires a certain dying to self. I recall the words of Christ: 'Whoever wants to save his life shall lose it; but whoever loses his life for my sake shall find it' (Mt 16:25). That seems to me to be one of the most fundamental things our Lord ever said about how we are to live as Christians. In this phrase we see that Christian life is a daily dying to self, but it is more than that. It is also a rising, for our Lord says that it is in losing life that we find life. It is in dying that we are reborn. There are, therefore, what I will call the two movements of Christian love. Wherever people are loving and unselfish, there are always these two movements, giving and receiving, losing and finding, dying and rising. These two movements are the very heart-beat of Christian love.

This observation corresponds with experience. Wherever people are unselfish and generous, we sense immediately that they have within themselves an inner strength and an inner peace. They have acquired something which the world cannot give. Worldly things grow by getting. Love grows by giving. The true 'democracy' of Christianity is here. All that Christianity has to give to the world comes to those who are loving and unselfish, whatever their education or social class. It is a matter ultimately, not of what we have, but of what we are.

Christ's Death and Resurrection

If that is the way of life which Christ preached, we can expect that he practised it as well. The whole course of his life on earth was spent in the service of others, but this loving way of life reached its climax at the end. There we find the two movements of Christian love lived out to the full in the two great final events of his time on earth, his death and his resurrection. In losing life he found life – for himself and for others.

But there is more. Christ's death and resurrection are not just the supreme example to us of what Christian life is. These two events are charged with an inner power. They are for us the providential watershed, the source of energy, from which the strength to follow Christ's way is to be channelled into our lives. If there is such a thing as Christian love with its two movements, then this is nothing less than the actual dying and rising of Christ working themselves out in our lives. Christ's dying and rising are not just events of two thousand years ago. They are mysteries constantly renewed and constantly continued in the daily dying and rising of Christians. If our lives are filled with crosses, as we daily die to ourselves in all kinds of ways, great and small, they are also filled with thousands of little Easters, as we rise with Christ to that peace and sense of fulfilment which only he can give (Phil 3:10f; 2 Cor 4:10f).

Celebrating a Way of Life

Turning now from Christian life to Christian worship, we are in a better position to appreciate the Eucharist as our principal celebration of the Christian way of life. A ritual that celebrates a way of life is a common human experience. We will recall how, in Red Square in Moscow every November, Russian communism used to celebrate a way of life built on state power. In Britain, when the Queen opens Parliament, the considerable ritual of the occasion implies a particular view of life in which privilege and tradition play a major role. Every Sunday Christians come to Mass to celebrate once more their way of life and to rededicate themselves to it. It is, as we have seen, a way of life centred not on power nor on privilege, but on love. It is a way in which Christ's dying and rising are a continuing presence amongst us, and so it is understandable that this dying and rising, present in one way in our daily lives, should be present in another way, a sacramental way, in our Eucharist.

One approach to understanding the Eucharist, in the light of what we have just said, is to see its two main parts as corresponding in a special way to the two great movements of Christian love. The two main parts of the sacrament are the great prayer of offering in the canon of the Mass and the great banquet of joy in holy communion. Each of these in turn can be seen to correspond to Christ's death and resurrection and so to the two movements of Christian love.

The Two Movements in Mass and Life

In offering the Eucharistic Prayer we think especially of Christ's self-offering on the cross, and so we endeavour to unite our self-offering with his by uniting ourselves with the Eucharistic Prayer in the Mass. In holy communion we receive the life of the risen Christ, and in this way we are united with the mystery of his resurrection. Thus the two movements of Christian love give us a pattern through which we can bind together three different aspects of the one mystery of Christian life:

a)   the dying and rising of Christ at the end of his life on earth;
b)   the dying and rising of Christians in the daily out-pouring of Christian love;
c)   the dying and rising of the body of Christ, Head and members, in the great oblation celebrated in the Eucharistic Prayer and in holy communion.

What we experience in our daily lives is what we bring to the Eucharist, there to express it, celebrate it and deepen it by plunging it into the great mystery of Christ's death and resurrection made present again in the Mass.

The reflection we have just made gives us a basic framework within which to approach the mystery of the Eucharist. The purpose of the third section of this book is to consider the main points involved in living our lives in a Eucharistic way. The Eucharist is such an important thing in itself that, when people try to live their lives Eucharistically, it brings about in them a certain spirit, a way of looking at life. Here we want to see what that spirit is.

> At all times we carry about in our bodies the dying state of Jesus, so that the life of Jesus may be made manifest in our bodies too; for always we who are alive are being given up to death for Jesus' sake, so that the life of Jesus may be made manifest even in our mortal flesh.
>
> (2 Cor 4:10-11)

29   THE MASS AS OFFERING

What is the Mass? It is a question easily posed, one I have put to many people at various times and places, and repeatedly I am taken aback by the blank faces with which my question is met. I am not talking of the reaction of unbelievers or of those who have fallen away from religious practice. I have in mind people who are faithful to the Mass and wish to be fully committed to all that it implies. Indeed it is not so much that they do not understand, but that they find it hard to put it into words. The emptiness in their eyes is a reflection more of confusion than of ignorance.

Yet that is not good enough! We need to be able to put the meaning of the Mass into some simple words. We need to be able to express, both to others and to ourselves, what we are doing when we go to Mass. Can we put it in a nutshell? I think we can. The Mass is *the occasion when we give our lives to God.* Daily Mass-goers will think of giving their day to him. Sunday Mass-goers will think of giving him their week. But always it comes back to that surrender of ourselves to the divine source of all life and meaning, from whom all blessings descend on our days and weeks and whole life long.

The Preparation of the Gifts

How then do we do that in the Mass? One thinks especially of that part of the Mass where the priest prepares the gifts that are to be offered. He brings before the Lord the bread resting on the paten. He pours wine and water into the cup. The bread and wine at Mass are signs of ourselves which we wish to give to God. As was explained in a previous chapter, by giving these to God we return to him our whole existence, in its good moments and its bad moments, for him to use as he wills within his plan for the world.

The Offering of the Gifts

The offering of these gifts takes place during the Eucharistic Prayer, when Our Lord transforms our gifts into his own, the Eucharistic body and blood. But as the priest prepares for that great act of offering, we, in our own minds, should be preparing ourselves and our offering. Mentally we should place on the paten ourselves, our day, our lives, together with the offering of the whole Church. From earliest times the drop of water poured into the cup has been seen in the Church as a special sign of the offering of the people, destined to mingle with the wine of Christ's sacrifice. As the celebrant raises the paten before the Lord, some like to see not just the priest's fingers holding the plate, but those of all the world, yellow and brown, black and white, and ours with theirs, holding the symbol of our united offering before the face of God.

Our Lord is never outdone in generosity. When we give to him, he gives to us in return – 'good measure, pressed down, shaken together and running over' (Lk 6:38) – but we know that, in a sense, our openness to him has normally to come first, if he is to be able to work in us. That is why our giving to him is so important, not as a way of putting a claim on God, but as a way of surrendering ourselves to his goodness and of removing from within ourselves the things that hinder the flow of grace.

Of course the significance of our giving does not end with the Mass. Indeed, as we come out from the Church, it is only beginning. The giving of our lives to God in the Mass has no meaning unless it is followed by our living out that self-gift in the life of every day. A person devoted to the Mass in this way is committed to living life sacrificially. By 'sacrifice' here we do not mean anything like the dramatic self-offering of the martyrs. We refer simply to the hundred thousand opportunities we have in our daily round of preferring others to ourselves, of being 'people for others', cooperative in the community, caring for the sick, considerate towards the poor, but above all playing our part in our own homes with patience, forgiveness and unselfishness.

The Breaking of Bread

Another part of the Mass where this spirit of sacrificial self-giving is expressed is at the breaking of the bread. Christ himself is the bread broken for our sakes in the gesture by which he prepares his body to be distributed in communion. In a somewhat similar way the person devoted to the Eucharist is to become bread in the hands of Christ, bread broken and eaten by others in the demands they make upon us. Just as the priest is told at his ordination to 'imitate what he celebrates,' so the same can be said of every Christian who participates in the breaking of bread. Bread broken is bread given, and we are the bread of Christ consecrated to being given to others in the day to day round of love and service.

In seeing the Mass in this way we have some answer to those who like to criticize believers for being Christians on Sundays only. If our Christianity is not a reality seven days a week, then clearly there is something wrong, but the fault is not in the Mass but in ourselves. The whole meaning of the Mass is wrapped up in that total offering of our lives to God. It is not for nothing that we speak of the Mass as sacrifice. The Mass, therefore, is the self-offering of each and of all, united now, through the paten and the cup, with the one abiding sacrifice of Christ.

> *I urge you therefore, by the mercy of God, to present your bodies as a living sacrifice to God, holy and pleasing to him, your spiritual worship.*
> (Rom 12:1)

30   EUCHARIST AND CALVARY

At the centre of every Eucharist stands the cross. We now take it for granted that the image of the crucified Saviour should be found over or near the Eucharistic table, but in itself it is a strange custom to place the emblem of such a brutal execution at the centre of our most sacred celebration. It seems, however, that we need this constant reminder of the event which made our Eucharist possible.

The Memorial of His Sacrifice
In a previous chapter the point was made that the Eucharistic way has to be a sacrificial way. The reason is that the Eucharist itself is sacrificial, based ultimately on the sacrifice of Christ on the cross. As well as the action of his executioners, inflicting cruel torments on Our Lord, there was also on Calvary Our Lord's own action, by which he offered up his sufferings to the Father for our sakes. The torments of Calvary are over, and Christ does not die in the Mass; but the action by which he offered them to the Father is with us still, and that is what is made present in every Eucharist. In the teaching of the Church, the Mass is the same sacrifice as that of the cross.

One of the key words for expressing this in the Eucharistic tradition is the word memory. 'Do this in memory of me,' said Our Lord (Lk 22:19), and people have applied this phrase especially to the *memory* of the cross. We must never forget how much it cost Our Lord to make the Eucharist possible. It is only because he poured out on the cross the last breath in his body and the last drop of his blood that he can give us his body and blood in the Eucharist under the veil of signs. Without that original giving the signs would have no meaning. In the middle ages they often thought of the Mass as a kind of passion-play in which all the details of Calvary were repeated. While this is not literally true and leaves the resurrection out of account, it can be a helpful idea from time to time, especially, for instance, during a season like Lent, to make the memory of the cross come alive for us again.

Making Sacrifice Meaningful Today
Christ had a dream. He had a certain vision of what life on this earth could be if people would only turn from their sin and selfishness and seek a new relationship with God. His dream was of a whole new community of people beginning here below the future kingdom of God. The community of the kingdom was the cause for which Christ went to his death. He sacrificed himself in order to make that community possible.

People sometimes question today whether the sacrificial aspect of the Eucharist can be made meaningful for our modern world. If one remains with a purely ritual notion of sacrifice, then the doubt has some point; but if this aspect of the Eucharist can be linked with the crucial role of self-sacrifice in the bringing about of Christ's dream, both in Christ's case and in our own, then the relevance of Eucharistic sacrifice will become clear once again. In any cause worthy of the name there is a price that has to be paid. In Christianity that price is self-denying service and self-sacrifice. In giving ourselves to others we are giving ourselves to God, and that is what we celebrate in the Eucharistic sacrifice. Through the Mass, however, God draws our self-giving into union with his Son's, for the one is to be the basis of the other.

To say that our approach to the Eucharist must be sacrificial does not mean that it must be tragic. Those devoted to the Eucharist are not expected to go around with long faces. Indeed Our Lord explicitly ruled such an idea out (Mt 6:16). Ordinarily we do not have to go looking for the sacrificial element in life. It usually finds us out before we find it, so that normally it is a case of accepting the crosses that come our way, accepting them as best we can, cheerfully if possible. After all, the sacrifice of the Lord is the gateway to the resurrection – and the Lord loves the cheerful giver (2 Cor 9:7)!

Signs of the Passion
There are times, such as Lent, or at moments of great sorrow, when it is helpful to be conscious of the memories of the Lord's Passion in the Mass. The principal basis for such reflection is, of course, Our Lord's own words which are recited at the consecration of every Mass. Here the Lord is clearly referring to Calvary when he speaks of his body broken and his blood poured out. As well as these words, there are the Eucharistic gifts themselves, the same body and the same blood, though now in a glorified state. Many have seen in the very fact that there are two species rather than one a reference to the separation of Christ's body and blood in death.

But each of the sacred species on its own can be seen as a reminder of Our Lord's death. With the sacred host there is not only the phrase with which it is consecrated: it is his body 'given for you'; there is also the ritual of the breaking of the host as the people sing, 'Lamb of God.' It reminds us of his body broken for us on the cross.

Then there is the special significance of the Eucharistic cup.
Though at another time this sign can be seen as a festive cup and
so related to the resurrection and the feast of the kingdom, but
at moments when we are thinking especially of Calvary in the
Mass our thoughts will inevitably turn to the content of the cup,
the very blood of Christ poured out on the cross. 'Can you drink
of the cup that I am to drink?' says Our Lord to us as he said to
James and John (Mt 20:22). St John Chrysostom remarks that
coming to drink of this cup in holy communion is like bringing
one's lips to the pierced side of Christ on the cross (Jn 19:34).

The Great Prayer of Offering
The offering of Christ to the Father on the cross is especially
close to us during the Eucharistic Prayer, for that is the great
prayer of offering in the Mass. This aspect of offering is
especially clear in the First Eucharistic Prayer, but of course it
is present in each of the canons that have been given to us, not
least in the Lord's own words at the consecration. There are
two moments in particular where Christ's self-offering on the
cross is brought before us with special vividness. The first is at
the elevation of host and cup, one after the other, at the
consecration. At this moment one might recall the words of
Christ about being lifted up on his cross: 'And when I am lifted
up from the earth, I shall draw all people to myself' (Jn 12:32).
This 'elevation' of Christ on the cross is repeated now in a
sacramental way in the Mass: Christ held up once again
between heaven and earth, interceding for us with the Father.

The second moment is the conclusion of the canon. There
the priest raises up host and cup together, each of them
solemnly reminding the Father of the pain of Christ's passion,
the bread of his affliction and the cup of his sufferings. This is
the high point of the great Eucharistic Prayer and the climax of
the aspect of offering in the Mass.

In Remembrance of Me

From all this we can conclude that it is important for the Lord that his death be remembered – both by the Father and by us. As was said earlier, we must never be unmindful of what it cost the Lord to make the Eucharist possible. His death is the ultimate proof of his love (Jn 15:13); and it is the same love which has given us the Eucharist, so that the evidence once given two thousand years ago on Calvary can become vivid and vital for every believer in the familiar ritual of the Mass.

From this too we have some answer to those young people who sometimes complain of their difficulty in relating to the Mass. When they make such remarks, it is not the time for their elders to take them to task for their lack of faith, but to seize the occasion as a moment of growth. Often it occurs at a time when young people are beginning to leave childhood behind and learning to be adults, to be not just receivers, but doers and givers. At that stage they must learn the key Christian lesson that the cause of Christ needs doers and givers also, and that, in keeping with that, the Mass is not just something we receive, but something we do. We must not be thinking only of what others can do for us, but rather of what we can do for others and for God. The difficulties of life are a part of life, but the Mass teaches us how we can turn them to good account by offering them up to God for others and for ourselves. In a nutshell that is what we do in the Eucharist, uniting our offering with that of Christ for the sake of our families, our friends and for all those who depend on us before God.

> *Receive, O Lord, the gifts which come from the revelation of your beloved Son, so that the oblation of your faithful people may pass over into the sacrifice of him who desired in his mercy to wash the world's sins away.*
>
> The Roman Missal

31   EUCHARIST AND RESURRECTION

When the apostles and the first disciples of Our Lord used to look back to those extraordinary weeks after his resurrection, one of their outstanding memories was of the joy they had in sitting down to table with him once again. Peter recalled it later: We are those, he said 'who ate with him and drank with him after he rose from the dead' (Acts 10:41). The common table was a focal point in the risen Lord's task of forming his community once more and in moulding them into a united body to continue his work in the world.

Like any Jewish teacher with his disciples, it would have fallen to Our Lord to say grace with them before and after their meals together. Grace before meals, as we saw in a previous chapter, was a ritual with bread; grace after meals was a ritual with wine. At the Last Supper Our Lord celebrated these rituals in the new form of the Eucharist. It seems almost unthinkable then that, after the resurrection, eating with them again in that same Upper Room, he did not continue to celebrate these rituals in his new way, bringing out the wonderful truth that through the death and resurrection, to which his new rituals point, something of the joy of the final kingdom of God had broken into their world.

Indeed the celebration of the resurrection seems to have been the first notion the disciples had of the Eucharist. To recognize the risen Lord in the breaking of bread was the experience of all in the Upper Room and not just of the two in the inn at Emmaus. The understanding of his death and of its place in the Eucharist was something that came more slowly to them. But before that, they had this astounding joy to celebrate: that the Lord was risen, victorious over death, and present to them in their worship.

The Heavenly Liturgy

After the weeks of the resurrection appearances, the risen Lord ascended into heaven, and the mystery of his glorification entered a new stage. Now there began that great heavenly liturgy described for us in the Letter to the Hebrews. At God's throne our great High Priest, in union with the whole assembly of heaven, is constantly interceding on our behalf, bringing the offering of his body and blood to its fulfilment. In celebrating the Eucharist the Church eventually came to realize that this heavenly liturgy is the ultimate reality behind our praise and worship here below (cfr Heb 12:22-24).

We in the Western Church are not as familiar with the thought of the heavenly liturgy as we might be, but we will never understand the way the prayers of the Church approach the Eucharist until we become more familiar with the heavenly priesthood of Christ. In this the Eastern Church has been much more consistent. This heavenly liturgy is the truth which sustains the rich ceremonial and sense of mystery which so mark the Eastern Mass. But even in the West the thought is not absent, and it is but the natural extension into liturgy of the truth of the resurrection and glorification of Christ. It comes to expression in every Mass, especially in the Preface when we say, Holy, Holy, Holy, in union with the angels and saints around the throne of glory (Apoc 4:8).

The Feast of the Kingdom

But the principal significance of the resurrection for our Eucharist lies in the way it gives us a glimpse of the goal, the great design which Christ carried in his heart as he instituted the Eucharist and went to his death. Christ had a dream, of which the parable in Mt 25:31-46 gives us a blue-print. He looked forward to a whole new community of people established on a whole new relationship between them and God. This was the cause for which he went to his death.

Indeed this community was to be the leaven spreading in the dough to which he compared the kingdom of God on earth (Mt 13:33). His design will reach its completion only at the end of time, when he sits down with Abraham and Isaac and Jacob and all the friends of God in the feast of the kingdom (Mt 8:11). In the Eucharist he has not only left us a ritual image of that final banquet, but by his resurrection has, as it were, brought it forward; and ever since the beginning of the Church it has been an element in that joy with which we are to celebrate the breaking of bread (Acts 2:46).

One of the earliest prayers of the liturgy, which has been preserved in the Aramaic of those early gatherings, is 'Maranatha,' meaning 'Come, Lord Jesus' (1 Cor 16:22; Apoc 22:20). It is a prayer on two levels. Firstly, it is a petition for the joy of his second coming in the kingdom of the end of time; but it is also a prayer for the anticipation of that joy by his presence in every Eucharist. To sum up we can say that, when the Eucharist is seen in the light of all this, there are three themes in particular which stand out: joy, community, kingdom.

The Eucharist and Joy

Every Eucharist must be an occasion of joy. Christ has conquered! That is the great message which rings out with the Easter bells, as Lent comes to an end and the Easter season begins. But it is true also of every Sunday and indeed of every Mass. The story of Jesus does not end on the cross. If it did, we would not be writing about him and the Eucharist would not exist. The very fact that we celebrate the Eucharist at all is a tribute to the truth that Jesus is risen. That is why every Eucharist is a feast of the Lord's resurrection. Indeed the resurrection is the reason why every Eucharist is a *celebration.* We are not puritans! In every Mass we like to sing; the ministers wear fine vestments; we like to have flowers, music, festive candles, incense, processions. It is all a way of celebrating that the Lord is risen! In some seasons of the year, or on some particular occasions such as a funeral, the note of joy will be more muted than at other times; but even in a Christian funeral the note of the resurrection cannot be suppressed. It is always there to some extent, to lessen our sadness and to give us strength.

The Eucharist and Community

Every Eucharist is also a celebration of community. In a previous chapter we mentioned the teaching of the Vatican Council that all education in community should take its origin in the Eucharist (*The Ministry and Life of Priests,* art. 6). From the history we outlined at the beginning of this chapter, Christian community is particularly associated with the resurrection. In his Passion the Shepherd was smitten and the sheep were scattered (cfr Mk 14:27). The only one who did not need redemption for himself died alone. But in the resurrection the Good Shepherd gathered together his scattered sheep, forming his community again around the table in the Upper Room, and that is what he continues to do in every Mass. The Eucharist is essentially about community because it is the risen Christ continuing to form his community around the common table. If we think especially of the sacrifice of Christ as we offer the Eucharistic Prayer, let us think especially of the resurrection of Christ when we join with others in holy communion.

The Eucharist and the Kingdom

Finally we must be mindful that the joy and community to which we refer, human as they are, are that and much more than that. Sometimes in our secular age, people have tried to turn our liturgies into nothing more than celebrations of

human togetherness. That empties our Eucharist of its
meaning and its mystery, and totally underestimates what it
cost Our Lord to make our Eucharist possible. By his death on
the cross Christ purchased nothing less than a new heaven and
a new earth (2 Pet 3:13). This is another name for the kingdom
of God, and it is this kingdom, inaugurated by Christ's
resurrection, which becomes present and actual in the
Eucharistic banquet. As evidence of that you might count the
number of times the kingdom is mentioned at Mass from the
'Our Father' on. This reflects the faith of the Church that in this
banquet we anticipate that 'feast in the kingdom of heaven' of
which the scriptures speak (Mt 8:11). In this light we can see the
Eucharist as a kind of bridge between the human community
of everyday living and the community of the kingdom at the
end of time. Maranatha! Come Lord Jesus! Truly the Eucharist
is for us the beginning of the new heaven and the new earth,
and the food and drink we share in it is the glorified body and
blood of a risen Saviour.

> *He never ceases from offering himself for us, and he constantly*
> *pleads our cause before you. Immolated once, he dies now no*
> *more, but always lives on as the one who was slain.*
> Preface from the Roman Missal

32   FAITH IN HIS PRESENCE

When the two disciples, who had walked with Our Lord to
Emmaus, looked back afterwards at their experience, they must
have realized that never again could they think of Jesus as
simply absent. The risen Lord is always present, in the Upper
Room, on the Emmaus road, beside the sea of Galilee, on top
of Mount Olivet, everywhere. One of the great fruits of
reflection on the resurrection of the Lord is a new appreciation

of this consoling mystery of his universal presence. Jesus is always at hand, even when we do not recognize him. He is all around us in the universe. He is in other people. He is within us.

Old Testament Presence

The presence of the Lord is one of the great themes of the Old Testament by which the teachers of Israel were unconsciously preparing for Christ. It began in the desert in a tent or tabernacle ('tabernacle' means 'tent') where Moses kept the Ark of the Covenant. This was called the Tent of Meeting, and there Moses would come to consult the Lord. In time Solomon built a permanent dwelling for the Ark. This was the temple, and the altar at the centre of the temple was considered to be God's throne – the Seat of Mercy, as it was called. There God dwelt with Israel and the people brought him their worship.

New Testament Presence

In the New Law the presence of the divinity is given a new centre in the person of Jesus. The phrase about the coming of the Word in the first chapter of John's gospel could be summed up, 'The Word pitched his tent in the flesh of Jesus' (cfr Jn 1:14). From now on that flesh is the tabernacle of God among the people. Christ is, in his own person, what the temple was for the Jews. All the comings and goings between heaven and earth are to pass through him (Jn 2:19-21).

For Christians, therefore, the first tabernacle of God is the flesh of Christ. When in the Middle Ages the Church began to develop its devotion to the body of Christ in the sacrament, it often built the place of reservation in the form of a tent, even if the material were stone or wood, and this place became the new 'tabernacle' of God. Just as the disciples at Emmaus learned their lesson about the divine presence from their experience on the road, so most of us learn it from our experience of the tabernacle.

As we will see in the following chapter, there are many ways in which Christ becomes present to us, but at the centre of them all, and maintaining our belief in all the others, stands the tabernacle. From here we learn, as Pope John Paul II put it, a whole sacramental style of living. This means that from the sacrament we build up an ever deeper sense of the closeness of God, that he is present behind all kinds of things, events and people in our lives. In him we live and move and have our being (Acts 17:28).

A Deeper Notion of Presence

Here we want to deepen our notion of what we mean by 'presence.' Presence is not only a term about space. A person can be right in front of you and yet be a million miles away, as school-teachers know to their cost. Space is only one aspect of presence. There is also the aspect of awareness in knowledge and in sympathetic love. In this way we come to see that there can be degrees of presence as people grow in understanding and in love with the person to whom they are present.

This also helps us to appreciate how, in its higher forms, presence should be mutual. It is one thing for Christ to be present to us in the tabernacle; it is another for us to be present to him. Indeed here we see one of the great purposes of the tabernacle. It is not just to bring his presence to us, since he is present to us already in so many ways; but this form of his presence is intended precisely to bring about our presence to him. It is really in view of this mutual sharing of presence that the reserved sacrament is called the sacrament of presence. Our mutual presence with the Lord in the tabernacle is a sign of, and help towards, that mysterious relationship of mutual 'abiding' which the fourth Gospel sees as one of the permanent fruits of the Eucharist (Jn 6:56).

Finally we discover here how the tabernacle fulfils a role which the Mass by itself cannot do. There is so much happening during Mass, and we are hopefully active in the liturgy in so many ways, that rarely during Mass do we have the peace and quiet to concentrate on the wonder of this mutual presence between Our Lord and ourselves. This then is what we can do more easily before the tabernacle. Perhaps the perfect expression of this comes in a well-known story from the life of the Curé of Ars. There was an old countryman whom the curé used to see frequently praying before the tabernacle. One day the curé asked him how he prayed at such times. The old man's answer contained it all in a phrase: 'I look at Him, and He looks at me.'

> *Anyone who eats my flesh and drinks my blood abides in me and I in that person* (Jn 6:56).

33   A Mystery Of Presence

When the Second Vatican Council came to speak of the Real Presence of Christ in the Eucharist, it did not add anything to what had been taught before about this mystery, but it did set it in a new light by placing it in a new context. The subject comes up in the Constitution on the Liturgy where the council gives us teaching on liturgical presence generally (*article* 7).

The council's main point is that there are several different ways in which God is really present to the people during the liturgy of the Mass. Before the council people would have associated the coming of Christ's presence in the Mass with the tinkling of the bell at the consecration. Now the Church wishes to draw our attention to the other ways in which Christ becomes present to us, including that by which he is already present from the beginning of the Mass in the people who gather in his name (cfr Mt 18:20).

The Many Ways of Real Presence
This doctrine was taken up by Pope Paul VI in his great
encyclical, The Holy Eucharist (*Mysterium Fidei*). Here he
expands on the lead given by the council. He lists no less than
seven different ways, both inside and outside the liturgy, in
which the Lord becomes present to his people. He is 'really
present' –

a)   in the Church praying;
b)   in the Church carrying out the works of mercy;
c)   in the Church preaching;
d)   in the Church exercising the authority it has from Christ;
e)   in the Church celebrating each and every sacrament;
f)   in the Church celebrating Mass, especially in the person of
      the ordained celebrant;
g)   in the consecrated host and cup.

The Holy Father insists that each of these modes of presence is
properly called 'real presence', but he considers that the last
one, that in consecrated host and cup, is 'the supreme form' of
presence. By this expression he wishes to underline a certain
difference in the modes of presence. In the other cases the
presence comes about through what is being done, but in this
instance it comes about through what the sacrament is.

Liturgy and Life
In approaching the truth about the Blessed Sacrament in this
way, the Church today is building on one of the great
suggestions of contemporary writers, namely that the meaning
of the seven sacraments will come home to us more deeply if
we keep in mind how each of them is related to the rest of life.
Though each of the sacraments has its own special value and
power, it is but a high point in a process that runs through life

generally. In a sense, all of life is sacramental. What occurs in the ritual of a sacrament is a consecration of a way of finding God in the bits and pieces of everyday.

His Presence in the Church

However, the instance of the Lord's presence, which is foundational for all the rest, is his presence in the Church. This is what was in mind when he said to the apostles just before his ascension, 'Behold I am with you always, until the end of time' (Mt 28:20). These words were spoken to emphasize that, though the days of their seeing him were coming to an end, he was in no sense withdrawing his presence from them. What he was withdrawing was the *visibility* of his presence, so that seeing might give way to believing. In future they would, if anything, be all the closer to him for knowing him more deeply through the mysterious ways of faith. The existence of the Church is the fundamental solution to the problem of distance between Christ and ourselves.

Once we have grasped that this problem of distance is already solved, then we can come to see that these various modes of presence are the ways in which this all-embracing presence of Christ in his Church enters into the various aspects of our lives. The Blessed Sacrament is not a means for establishing a presence across a spatial divide. To be confronted with the Eucharistic body of Christ is rather a uniquely moving invitation to enter more deeply into a presence, which is indeed all around us, but of which we think too little.

A Celebration of Presence

Conscious, therefore, of the many ways in which we enjoy the presence of Christ in our daily lives, we can come to see the Mass precisely as a celebration of this multiple gift of presence, experiencing in the ritual, as we celebrate it, the several modes of presence proper to the liturgy. Indeed the whole celebration may be seen as a mounting mystery of presence, leading up to and away from the central action of the Mass.

Leading up to that centre there are a number of ways in which Christ becomes really present. He becomes present, from the beginning, in the congregation gathering in his name; he is present in the liturgy of the word, not only when the word of God is read, but even as it is preached; he is present in the priest, who, in virtue of the sacrament of Orders, acts in the person of Christ; and so we come to the greatest moment of presence, when Christ gives his very self to the Father under the signs of our gifts.

Leading away from that centre we have the celebration of holy communion. Here Christ is present in one way in the host, in another way in the cup. Christ is present in the communicants who receive him. He is present in the sacrament reserved in the tabernacle. He is present in a new way in all the people who go out from Mass with the grace of God renewed within them; and finally, through those very people and their Mass together, Christ becomes present more fully in the world.

Learning from this Mystery

One of the results of this teaching is, as was said above, that it levels down our approach to the key truth that in the Eucharist bread and wine become Christ's body and blood. Familiarity with these other ways in which Christ is really present prepares us for the wonder of his presence in host and cup. If Christ is present in our gatherings as he was among his own people, then we can expect him to renew among us the kind of signs he worked in Cana of Galilee and in the multiplication of the loaves – and that is what he does in the Eucharist.

Human beings have many sides to them. This multitude of ways in which Christ becomes present to us during Mass reflects

Our Lord's desire to become present to us in all the different aspects of the kind of people we are. Each of these ways helps the other ways, and so the reality of the presence of the Lord to us is intended to become ever deeper and more all-embracing. In a previous chapter we quoted Pope John Paul II on a sacramental style of living flowing from the Eucharist. For people devoted to the Eucharist the presence of God in their lives should eventually become second-nature. Christ becomes as real to them, if not more real, than the person next door. We have all met people like that. It is a great grace to be given, and a great joy to see. Indeed it is one of the main things which the Eucharist is all about.

> *In the Eucharist he has made himself our support and company on our pilgrim way.*
> St Ignatius Loyola (d. 1556)

34   TABERNACLE DEVOTION

One of the remarkable developments in recent years in a number of countries has been the rebirth of devotion to the reserved sacrament. Often it is just a question of people spending time before the tabernacle, but in many places it has taken the form of periods of exposition, during which people come to pray in organized groups. It is especially with this development in mind that this chapter has been drawn up as a reflection on how such periods of prayer might be spent. We must acknowledge that to many Christians today this kind of prayer does not make much sense. Ultimately it is a matter of the heart.

The Offered Christ

The Second Vatican Council gave us one of our main clues about our approach to the reserved sacrament when it said,

'The most holy Eucharist holds within itself the whole spiritual treasure of the Church, namely Christ himself, our passover and our living bread' (*The Ministry and Life of Priests*, art. 5). As our passover and our living bread, Christ will always be the one who, at a certain point of space and time, offered himself for each of us out of a unique love (Jn 15:13).

In this reflection we might be helped by a thought from St Robert Southwell (d. 1595). Robert was an English priest, poet and martyr during the reign of Elizabeth I. In one of his poems he wrote as follows:

> He loved our love more than his life,
> and love with life did buy.

Robert's special response to that love was the gift he made of his own body in surrendering it to the executioner's sword.

On our altars our Lord points to that very body once given for us on Calvary as the price he paid for our love. The body on the cross and the body in the Eucharist are one. Indeed around every tabernacle we could write the words, 'This is my body given for you.' When we pray before the Blessed Sacrament we want the message contained in those familiar words of the Lord to come home to us. Then we will want to make our response, and the first response we can make is our very prayer itself and the time we give to it before the sacrament. Our offering him our bodily presence is a way for each of us, in our turn, to say to him, 'This is my body given for you.' He is present to us, and we are present to him.

To deepen this thought we might reflect at this point on Christ's desire to be with us. Our being before him is an expression of our desire to be with him; but great as our desire may be, it is as nothing to the desire that he has to be with us. By bringing ourselves before him, we are letting him give rein to his desire to be with us, person to person, heart to heart.

In making this response of prayer to Christ, many will wonder about what kind of prayer we might turn to. Many will have their own favourite forms of prayer, and these, of course, will be the first to come to mind. Others might have some familiar book of prayers or reflections, such as this one. Another possibility is to turn to the Bible. There we have, first of all, the book of the psalms, the great prayers of Israel once used by our Lord, our Lady and the Apostles. The following psalms might be found helpful: 22(23); 26(27); 33(34); 41(42); 62(63); 83(84); 94(95); 99(100); 115(116); 138(139); 144(145).

Another way in which to pray is by reading slowly and prayerfully selected scenes from the Gospels, such as Mk 6:34-44; Lk 10:38-42; Lk 24:13-35; Jn 21:1-19. Then there are the great discourses of our Lord in the fourth Gospel, chapter 6 about the Bread of Life, and chapters 13 to 17 which give us our Lord's farewell discourse at the Last Supper. Texts which have had a special influence on Eucharistic devotion are, Jn 6:54-58; Jn 14:12-26, especially vv. 20-23; Jn 15:1-12; Jn 17:20-26; Apocalypse 3:20.

The Church

A second main line of prayer before the sacrament is the thought of the Church. From St Paul on, the Eucharistic bread has reminded people of the mystery of the Church (1 Cor 10:17). As long ago as the third century St Cyprian put it this way:

> When the Saviour takes the bread that is made from the coming together of many grains and calls it his body, he shows the unity of our people, of which the bread is the sign.

The Eucharistic Christ is the Christ of the Church. He is there to build up the Church, his mystical body, and the sacrament is, in the words of the Gospel, the flesh of Christ for the life of the world (Jn 6:51). There is a power going out from the Eucharist to help transform the world. The body that is the Eucharist makes the body that is the Church, not only through Mass and holy communion, but also through the power of the reserved sacrament.

In response to this concern of Christ for the Church, our concern for others becomes an important theme of our prayer before the Eucharist. In the first place there is intercession for others, offering to Christ our devotion as a way of gaining for others as well as for ourselves an increase of faith and grace. Before the Blessed Sacrament we might review our relations with others and how we are living out that commitment to others which must be part of every Mass. We must always bear in mind the stern words of St John, 'He who does not love his brother whom he can see cannot love the God he has not seen' (1 Jn 4:20).

Because this kind of prayer is such a personal act, it runs the danger of becoming turned in on self, and that would be a contradiction of what this devotion is all about. The sacrament is the sacrament of love, and love is always about other people. We might think again of St Thérèse of Lisieux, who learned by her life of prayer to become Patroness of the Missions without ever having to leave her convent. She came to see, as she put it, that 'love is all,' and that her vocation was to be love at the heart of the Church. Like Thérèse in her prayer, we want to think of others as well as of ourselves, of our families, our friends, and of all those, the quality of whose lives before God depends on us.

The Bread of Healing

A third aspect of the sacrament which can help our prayer is the thought that this is the bread of healing. When this custom of reserving the Eucharist began, one of the main reasons was for the communion of the sick. There is a strong tradition in the

Church, which we meet especially in the Post-Communion prayers of the Mass, that the Eucharist has a healing power for both soul and body. While this power works especially through holy communion and viaticum, one can also think of the healing power of Christ radiating out from the reserved sacrament as a remedy for the wear and tear of daily life.

In this line of thought we might spend some time praying over some of the great scenes of healing in the New Testament, such as Mk 1:21-34; 2:1-12; 5:21-43; 9:14-29; Lk 7:11-17; 17:11-19; Jn 5:1-15; 9:1-41. The Old Testament speaks of the sun in the sky as having healing in its rays or wings (Mal 3:20). The sun at the centre of the solar system has often been seen as an image of the Blessed Sacrament. This is why the monstrance for the host has often been shaped like the sun. The sacrament on our altars is like the sun in the sky with healing in its rays.

The Prayer of Silence

After all these suggestions, there is one final one, which is the simplest of all: adoration by silence. More often than not, it is enough just to be there and to say nothing. 'Be still and know that I am God,' said the Lord in Psalm 45(46). As we have seen, the highest form of presence is something between two persons: he present to me, and I present to him. Just be glad to be there. One might recall the words of Christ in Mt 11:28-30, or just no words at all, as with the friend of the Curé of Ars, quoted in an earlier chapter: 'I look at him, and he looks at me.'

> *To believe in love is everything. It is not enough to believe in truth. We must believe in love, and love is our Lord in the Blessed Sacrament.*
> St Peter Julian Eymard (d. 1868)

35   THE SACRED HEART AND THE EUCHARIST

What scenes in the Gospel come to your mind when we speak of Jesus as the Sacred Heart? Many people will think of the events on Calvary or at the institution of the Eucharist, but one scene worth considering is that occasion before the feeding of the five thousand people in the desert, which we find described in Mk 6:30-44. Our Lord looked at the people. They were like sheep without a shepherd, and our Lord was stirred within himself. 'His heart was filled with pity,' is the way one version[9] puts it, and it is surely right, for at this point the Gospel is referring to all that we sum up in the name, the Sacred Heart.

What does it mean to say that Jesus is a man with a heart? The meaning is at once familiar and profound. His heart expresses not only that he is divine love made visible, but also that the deep red blood of human emotion runs in his veins in no way different from the way it runs in ours. Confronted with human suffering, he is moved to compassion. At the sight of injustice his fist is clenched. The death of his friends brings tears to his eyes.

Jesus Cares

If ever there was someone who cared, it was Jesus. Once launched on his public life, he became involved in many of the great social issues of his day, especially the struggle against poverty and sickness, and even against oppressive forms of religious teaching. At revolutionary nationalism he drew the line, since divisiveness and physical force were not his way. Nevertheless his involvement won him few friends in high places. They still saw him as a threat to the established order of things, and so they put him to death. At that point Jesus' life-

---

9. *Good News for Modern Man*, London: Collins 1966.

work was only beginning. The multitudes, which had so moved his heart when he found them without a shepherd, were still shepherdless when he was taken from them. But our Lord could look at them, not only as the compassionate healer of Galilee, but also as Son of God with a universal mission; and so his heart was moved in another way.

The point I wish to make might best be illustrated by shifting our camera for a moment from the scene of Christ with the people of his day to some of the harrowing scenes of our own time which our television sets have brought before us in recent years: the people dying in the Ethiopian famine; the Kurds scattered on the wintry mountain-slopes to escape Saddam Hussein; the unforgettable catastrophe of the Rwandan genocide.

From reading the Gospel in depth we know that what ultimately moves the heart of Christ is the physical and spiritual hunger of all the multitudes of all time. Our Lord, however, was limited by the conditions of time and space. He could not remain on earth in the ordinary way to care for all those people himself, so what he did was to establish a group of people who would continue his work among them. It was like in the Gospel story, where he himself did not go round to each of the five thousand in the desert but gave the food to his disciples, who then distributed it on his behalf (Mk 6:41). This group that he established was the Church, the body of Christ, a community filled with his presence. We, the Church, then, are his hands and his feet, charged to continue that mission which was so close to his heart. In these days where people often have problems with the very notion of a Church, it is important to see that the Church of Christ is born, not simply as an instrument of teaching or administration, but as part of the plans of Christ's heart to be present to all the problems, both physical and spiritual, of the multitudes of this world.

The Body of Christ

You and I are his hands. Whenever we reach out to help a fellow human being, whether in the dramatic ways of a Mother Teresa, or in the unsung ways of parents with their children, teachers with their pupils, workers with those around them, ultimately this is Christ alive in us, and we are helping him in the 'plans of his heart' – Ps 32(33):11. You and I are his feet. Wherever we go to bring to others the good news of salvation, whether in the explicit ways of priests and teachers, or in the implicit ways of all who endeavour to bear witness to Christ by the integrity of their lives, ultimately this is Christ in us, and he is advancing in the world through us.

The doctrine of the Body of Christ is one of the most wonderful doctrines in the Christian faith. It is, as we saw in the previous chapter, the foundation of our teaching on his continuing presence among us, and now we see it as a masterpiece of his love. Ever since the Ascension, Christ has not been visible here below in his own flesh, but he is visible through us, his Body, and in us he lives on to bring about here below his civilisation of love. But Christ is not only the head of the Church, his body. He is also its heart, and that is part of what we mean by calling him the Sacred Heart. At the heart of the Church there beats the Heart of Christ. This is the source of whatever love and energy circulates in us from him.

The Challenge

This truth is not only our consolation. It is also for us a challenge. By our service of others, and by our confession of the faith, we extend into our world the labours of his hands and feet. But are we also for others an extension of his heart? Do they experience through us something of that goodness and compassion and forgiveness which moved in his breast and should be stirring in ours? That is what we mean by saying that the truth of Christ's heart issues a real challenge. The heart of Christ speaks to us, not only of all that we receive from him, but also of all that we do through him, and ultimately of all that we are to be for him. He is the Vine, and we are the branches. He is the head, and we are his members. He is the heart, and we are to be the out-reach of his love in a world that seems to need it more and more.

The Bread of Life
Going back to that day in the desert with which we began this chapter, if the love of Christ's heart was the main-spring of all he did for the crowd, we should notice that the Eucharist was part of what he had in mind on that day. The multiplication of the loaves, after all, was a preparatory sign of the sacrament, showing us that the Eucharist is part of the plans of his heart, part of his response to the plight of a people languishing in the desert. As we have seen in this and other chapters of this book, the Eucharist is to be the source of that life in us, which will enable us to be his hands and feet and heart in the world of our time.

> *There is so much hunger in the world, one realises that if God were to come down on earth, he would do so in the form of bread.*
> Mahatma Gandhi

36   SCHOOL OF CHARITY

Several years ago audiences throughout the world were greatly drawn to a television programme in which the late Malcolm Muggeridge interviewed Mother Teresa of Calcutta. Having talked with her of the ceaseless labours of her sisters and herself to serve the poor, with many close-ups of them in the streets and in the hospitals, Muggeridge wondered where they got the energy for it all. I will always remember how Mother Teresa answered like a shot. What made it possible for them to face the day was getting up early and going to Mass and holy communion. That was for them the main source of their energy and their love.

This programme appeared at a providential moment, for it was during the period after the Second Vatican Council, when many Catholics were in a state of some confusion about their faith. They were seeing some old and well-tried practices being dropped and they had not yet achieved a balance in the new ways of thinking and acting. With familiar forms of prayer under question, one sometimes heard remarks like, 'My work is my prayer,' or, 'I have no need of the tabernacle, I find God in my neighbour.'

Sacrament of Presence

The last remark in particular shows just how confused people can be, especially when you think of the statement of Mother Teresa quoted above. Thankfully one hears this kind of confused remark less often now than thirty years ago. But if something of that feeling is still around, one should make one thing clear. While we insist that there are several ways in which God is really present to his people, there is no rivalry between the various forms of presence. The whole point is that each kind of presence helps the other: God present in the universe, Christ present in our neighbour, the Spirit present within us; and in the middle of all these manifestations of the divine presence stands the Eucharist. It is the sacrament of presence, the centre of all the other kinds of presence, and the source of our response to each of them. Our devotion to Christ's Eucharistic presence should make us more aware of and responsive to all these different ways in which Christ is really present to his people.

This is particularly true of our awareness of the presence of Christ in those around us. There is a special bond between the presence of Christ in the sacrament and his presence in our neighbour. The Eucharist is at once a celebration of both forms of presence, since the body and blood of Christ are offered to all who come to this table. The sacrament, after all, is the great banquet to which all the friends of God are invited from the highways and bye-ways (Lk 14:23) to be nourished with this divine food. The presence of Christ passes from the sacrament into the lives of all who come to worship here. The whole point of there being one table around which we gather at the Eucharist is to manifest how the celebration is essentially the act of a community, for a community and by a community. I cannot recognize Christ's presence here for me without being aware of his being present here for others also.

Sacrament of Love

Then the Eucharist is the sacrament of love. First of all, it is the sacrament of God's love for us, that love by which he sent his Son to die for us while we were still sinners (Rom 5:8). It makes no sense to be part of this sacrament of love if I am not trying to be a loving person in my own life as well; and as we know from 1 Jn 4:20, the test of my loving God whom I cannot see is the love I have for my neighbour whom I do see. To put it bluntly: we cannot be devoted to the Eucharist without being devoted to the neighbour. This is why Pope John Paul II said so finely that the Eucharist is a school of charity, a school of love.

But our devotion to the Eucharistic presence does not let us forget that this mystery of love is immersed in a mystery of presence. It is not just a question of doing good, but of doing it because of a presence. As Christ is present in one way in the Eucharist, so is he present in another way in the neighbour. The one teaches us about the other.

However there is a difference between the two modes of presence. In a previous chapter the point was made that, in its higher forms, presence is mutual. In other words, the way we respond to the presence is, in a sense, part of the presence; it is what releases into our lives the power of that presence. But each mode of presence calls for its own mode of response. The fitting response to Christ's presence in the sacrifice of the Mass is active participation in the liturgy. The fitting response to Christ's presence in the tabernacle is prayer, worship and adoration. The way to welcome Christ's presence in other people is not that I should genuflect when passing them but that I should attend to them and serve them. Experience shows that, as in the case of Mother Teresa and her sisters, the more my love and service is rooted in my devotion to the Eucharist, the more thorough and enduring it will be.

Action and Contemplation

In this point too we can see the difference between the place of the Mass in our lives and the place of devotion to the Blessed Sacrament. Sometimes people talk and act today as though the new liturgy has room only for the liturgy of the Mass and that devotion to the Blessed Sacrament belongs to another age. This is greatly to underestimate the difference between the two forms of worship and how each helps the other. There is no rivalry between them. The liturgy of Mass is a moment for active participation, thereby expressing our commitment to being active in the service of our neighbour. But if we are all action and never stop to think, we will remain on the surface of things. There is need also for quieter moments, times of contemplation, and that is what devotion to the reserved sacrament is all about. What Christ is looking for in the tabernacle is our prayerful response, and this it is which releases into our lives the power which his presence holds for us.

As was remarked in a previous chapter, there is so much going on during Mass that we cannot take it all in at the time. We need every so often to enter into ourselves and to reflect on all that the Lord is doing in us in his liturgy and in our lives generally; and where better to enter more deeply into the fruits of the Eucharist than in the presence of that reserved sacrament which is itself one of the fruits of the liturgy? The most important experience of the Eucharist remains for us our Mass with holy communion. Nothing can ever equal what the Lord does within us when he binds us to himself in holy communion; but once this has taken place, then our coming before the reserved sacrament is a way of 'fanning into a flame' (cfr 2 Tim 1:6) the graces we have received at our last sharing in the banquet of his love.

> Divine love in man needs a centre of life if it is to become habitual. The best centre is Jesus in the Blessed Sacrament.
> St Peter Julian Eymard

37   A Way of Love

All the sacraments are sacraments of love, but none more so than the Eucharist. The Eucharistic way of faith has to be a way of love. At first this statement seems too obvious, but the reality is not as obvious as one might think. There is a true and a false way of understanding it, depending on where you begin. Many modern people begin here below with our concern for human community. From there they build upwards, dwelling on the Eucharist as a banquet and easily falling into the mistake of seeing the Mass as simply a celebration of human togetherness, which Christ is then expected to accept.

Truly to understand the depths of love contained in this sacrament, one has to begin 'from above.' The builders of the tower of Babel, in Gen 11:1-9, began from below, and see what happened to them! The Eucharistic mystery begins in God and descends from the mystery of the divine Trinity. If one wanted an image with which to begin one could not do better than the famous Russian icon by Rublev: the Three Persons seated at a table, bending towards one another in a mystic union. The love contained in the Eucharist is as deep as the Trinity itself.

The Trinity Shares Itself

If there is one word which goes to the root of what love means, it is the little word 'sharing.' This notion has been Eucharistic from the beginning, being the key idea in the familiar word 'communion'. The life of love within the Trinity is a life of a mysterious eternal communion, as each of the three persons shares with the others what each one has and is.

At a certain point in our past this mystery of love overflowed upon us. We could not have been further from love and sharing at the time, locked as we were into our sinfulness and selfishness. But the wonder of divine love lies in this, that it was precisely in our sins that they loved us and decided to share their life with us, sending us the Second Person to be a human being in our midst. 'For God so loved the world, that he gave his only-begotten Son' (Jn 3:16). 'God commends his love for us in that it was while we were still sinners that Christ died for us' (Rom 5:8). 'In this is love, not that we loved God, but that he himself loved us and sent his own Son to be the atonement for our sins' (1 Jn 4:10).

Christ's life on earth is the extension of the divine life into our world. When the time came for him to return to the Father, the manifestation of divine love surpassed itself. Not content with having demonstrated his love on earth, reaching a climax in his death and resurrection, Almighty God devised yet a further extension of his love by instituting the Eucharist. Through this sacrament the whole mystery of divine love, embodied in Christ, would be extended into the 'here and now' of our churches and our liturgy. Through this sacrament the mystery of divine sharing would reach right into our lives.

Sacrifice of Love

First of all, through the Eucharist God still gives his Son as a sacrifice that takes our sins away. Not by a new Calvary, not by repeating Calvary, but by the mystery of a sacramental presence, the offering of Christ on the cross becomes actual amongst us, inviting us to enter into it in our turn and to share ourselves with him. Our freely entering into the movement of Christ's self-offering, by offering ourselves in the Mass with him, is our first response of love to the mystery of Eucharistic sharing.

Banquet of Love

But there is more! Not content with the making present of his sacrifice, the Lord went even further and brought the wonder of divine sharing to an extraordinary climax in the mystery of the banquet. Here we see divine love surpass itself yet again, as the Lord gives himself to all and to each. The love by which he died for each of us on the cross is the same love by which he gives himself to each of us in holy communion. The one is a kind of proof of the other.

Our second response of love is to give ourselves to Christ when we receive him in holy communion. He gives himself to us; let each of us give ourselves to him, so that each of us can learn to say with St Paul, 'I live now, not I, but Christ lives in me' (Gal 2:20). This marks yet a new level in the mystery of Eucharistic sharing.

School of Love

A third level comes when we reflect that, as well as giving himself to each of us, Christ is giving himself to others as well. All the friends of God are brothers and sisters of Christ, people for whom he died and in whom he wishes to live for ever. In a previous chapter it was pointed out, quoting Pope John Paul II, that the Eucharist is a school of charity, and so this third level of sharing gets a special meaning as we come out of the church and return to our daily lives. All that we share with one another in the comings and goings of everyday, sharing these things in a spirit of love and self-giving, all this can be seen as a fruit of the Eucharist and a fulfilment in practical living of a mystery that has its origins in the Trinity itself.

That then is what we mean by the title of this chapter, a way of love based on the Eucharist. The love in question is, first of all, that which exists in God and overflows on us. Our love comes about, not as the achievement of any natural goodness, but only as a response to a love from another world, the love coming from the divine Three themselves. To this we respond, and our response keeps on growing upwards and outwards in two directions, reaching up to God and reaching out to others. Far from being a work of a mere holy togetherness, it is itself a creation of God's love, shot through with the presence and power of a mystery from beyond ourselves, a mystery constantly nourished by the Eucharist's incomparable gifts. The following words from St Paul surely form a fitting conclusion to the account we have given.

> (I pray) that Christ may live in your hearts through faith, so that, rooted and grounded in love, you may, with all the saints, be strengthened to take in the breadth and length and height and depth; and that, knowing the love of Christ which is beyond knowledge, you may be filled with all the fullness of God.
>
> (Ephes 3:17-19)

38   THE MASS OF THE MARTYRS

It is only a few years ago that the world was shocked to learn of the death of Oscar Romero, Archbishop of San Salvador in

Central America, murdered by a right-wing death-squad while he was in the very act of saying Mass. This event underlined once again the age-old connection between martyrdom and the Mass. In the history of the faith nearer home, there are many stories which bear witness to the same bond.

Some Irish Martyrs
During the reign of Elizabeth I, Maurice McKenraghty, a native of Kilmallock, Co. Limerick, was a priest and chaplain to the Earl of Desmond, who had rebelled against the Queen. Late in 1583 Maurice was discovered and thrown into jail in Clonmel. Eighteen months later he was still in prison, when a local man of some substance, Victor White, bribed the jailer to let Fr Maurice come to his house to say Mass on the occasion of Easter 1585. This was arranged, and the priest was in Victor's house, ministering the sacraments, when the jailer changed his mind and betrayed them to Sir John Norris, the Lord President of Munster, who happened to be in Clonmel at the time. The priest was arrested, tried and summarily hanged, drawn and quartered for his devotion to the faith and to the Mass. He was not the first to meet that fate in that cause, nor would he be the last.

In the following century, when Cromwell descended on the country, his hostility to the Mass was even more pronounced. In 1649 he declared to the citizens of New Ross, 'I meddle not with any man's conscience, but if by liberty of conscience you mean a liberty to exercise the Mass ... that will not be allowed of.' Nor was it.

Fr John Kearney, a Franciscan and native of Cashel, was captured in his native town in March 1653. When brought before the authorities at Clonmel, the charge against him was that of saying Mass and administering the sacraments. He was hanged at Clonmel within the month, having declared from the scaffold that he was condemned because of the Mass. In the same month, Fr William Tirry, an Augustinian, was discovered vested for Mass in the house of a relative in Fethard, Co. Tipperary. He was hanged at Clonmel on the second of the following May. These three priests, with fourteen companions, were beatified by Pope John Paul II in 1992.

The Church of the Catacombs
Behind these stories lies a long Christian tradition which sees a value in the Mass greater than life itself. Similar stories can be found in the annals of the early persecutions. There was St Justin and his companions, discovered at Mass in Rome in the middle of the second century. 'We are Christians,' they said, 'and we do not sacrifice to idols.' At that they were beheaded. Similarly the martyrs of Abitina in North Africa, discovered at Mass one Sunday in the early fourth century. To the magistrate one of them said, 'We cannot live without our Sunday Mass.' In Rome they still point out the underground catacomb where some of the early martyred popes are buried. There we read how in the year 257 AD the Pope of the day, Sixtus II, was celebrating Mass with a group of deacons when the persecutors arrived. The worshippers were all brought before the magistrates and summarily put to death. In that setting the link between Mass and sacrifice was clear, sealed by the blood of Christians.

The Ideal Christian
In the early Church this connection was never in doubt. To give one's life for Christ was seen as the summit of Christian faith. The martyrs were the ideal Christians, and the connection was always present in the way they thought about the Mass. Since the Mass is the celebration of what Christian life is, the martyr is inevitably seen as the one who lives out the mystery of the

Eucharist to the full. As a prayer of the liturgy puts it, the Eucharist contains the sacrifice from which all martyrdom draws its origin.[10] A similar thought lies behind the First Eucharistic Prayer, with its two great lists of apostles and martyrs. In particular we should notice the phrase that introduces the second of these lists: 'For ourselves too we ask some share in the fellowship of your apostles and martyrs, with John the Baptist, Stephen, Matthias, Barnabas...' This is a petition which should give us pause before we make it our own.

A Sermon of St Augustine

The connection is well captured in a sermon of St Augustine, which he preached on the feast of St Laurence, the martyred deacon of Rome. At that time deacons had two main roles, one was to care for the poor on behalf of the Church, the other was to administer the chalice in the celebration of the Mass. Both roles prepared Laurence for the ultimate sacrifice of his life. As Augustine put it, in administering Christ's blood to the faithful he had learned to pour out his own blood for Christ as his ultimate gesture in the service of others.

The text St Augustine took for his sermon is noteworthy: 'In this have we come to know love, that Christ laid down his life for us, and we ought to lay down our lives for the brethren' (1 Jn 3:16). In this verse, says Augustine, the apostle was expounding the mystery of the Eucharist. His insight is a kind of circle. Our Lord's self-gift in the Mass challenges any responsive Christian to a life of unselfishness – what is sometimes called the white martyrdom of the service of others. Normally a life-time of such love of neighbour has to go before the grace and privilege of martyrdom are given. With the red martyrdom of death this life-time of love of our

---

10.   Prayer over the Gifts in Latin, the feast of Saints Cosmas and Damian, September 26.

brothers and sisters reaches its high-point in the final act of surrender for the sake of our Elder Brother, Christ. In this way the meaning of our Lord's gift of his body and blood in the Eucharist is carried to its ultimate and awesome fulfilment in the human life of the believer. The challenge of Christian life and of the Eucharist has come full circle.

Martyrdom is not a prospect for the majority of us today. Indeed for most of us the thought of it, if it has any reality at all, can only fill us with confusion. At the same time, it is good to be reminded from time to time that the faith we celebrate in the Eucharist is a value which comes to us only because people died for it in the past, and it is one for which people continue to give their lives even today. The best the majority of us can do is to hope we would be faithful if the question were ever to arise, even though the very thought of it fills us with fear. However as well as the red martyrdom of the ultimate sacrifice there is the white martyrdom of the daily service of others. This too is part of the meaning of the Eucharist. In the words of an ancient prayer already referred to, we are called on, in our ordinary lives, to imitate what we celebrate.

> *Look down, almighty God, on the gifts we offer and grant that we who are carrying out the mysteries of the Lord's passion may imitate what we celebrate: We ask this through Christ our Lord. Amen.*
> The Roman Missal

39   HOST AND CUP

In recent years Catholics have become more aware of the fact that the Lord instituted the Eucharist in two species, host and cup. For so long the Eucharistic Cup had been reserved to the clergy that the ordinary faithful hardly used to give it a thought, but in this, as in so many things, the Second Vatican Council brought about a change. Ever since that time the use of the cup for the communion of all has been gradually increasing among us. This seems only to be welcomed, since the Lord himself makes no distinction of persons in saying, 'Take and eat ... take and drink.'

The Origin of the Two Species

However this development raises a question in people's minds as to the meaning of the rite and as to why there are two species at all. The answer to the last question comes in two stages. First of all we should recall a point made in an earlier chapter, that the Lord did not establish the Eucharist from zero. At the Last Supper he took the familiar rituals over bread and wine by which the Jews said grace before and after meals. In taking them he transformed them by turning them into a sign of his self-offering in death and resurrection. Already in themselves these rituals lent themselves to the notion of offering. Like a hand shielding us from the sun, the Lord used these rituals to veil from us the brutal reality of his death and the awesome mystery of his resurrection, but the kernel of these two events, the victorious self-offering of Christ, is the reality which lies contained within the Eucharistic rite.

Signs of His Sacrifice

Having then two species, bread and wine, from the Jewish origins of the sacrament, the Lord took advantage of their significance when he transformed the meaning of the rituals and filled them with his Holy Spirit. Since the Eucharist is centred on the sacrifice of Christ, as Jesus' words of consecration already make clear, it was fitting that the two species be used to refer to the two main elements in any Jewish sacrifice, the flesh and blood of the victim. The fact that there are two species rather than only one helps to spell out the fact that this is not just any offering but the offering of a human life to the point of death. The offering of his body into the hands of the executioners was the way the Lord handed himself over to death. The offering of his blood only makes clear what is already implicit in the offering of his body, namely that, in giving himself, he goes to the ultimate, to the last drop of his blood. 'Having loved his own who were in the world, he loved them to the end' (Jn 13:1). The two species therefore help to bring out that the Eucharist contains Christ's self-offering on the cross out of a love that knows no bounds.

These two species call attention to themselves at two points of the Mass in particular: firstly during the Eucharistic Prayer, when we see host and cup being consecrated and offered; secondly at holy communion, when both species are consumed, especially if both are administered to the faithful. At both moments, as we have seen, the two species underline that this is a *sacrifice* that we are involved in, and that even our communion is communion in a sacrifice, with all the commitment that entails. It is not just a soothing experience of togetherness!

Each Species Has Its Meaning

What we have said so far helps us to understand the general meaning of communion under both kinds, but each species has its own special significance which should make us more aware of particular graces and fruits associated with that species. First of all, however, we should be clear that we receive Christ, whole and entire, body, blood, soul and divinity, under either species by itself. This means that all essential grace is offered to us whether we receive under one kind or under two. But each species has its own particular meaning and its own incidental fruits.

Various ways have been proposed for understanding this difference between the two species. In the middle ages they often associated the host with the body and the cup with the soul, but this does not seem to be quite biblical. Another manner of approach is to relate the host in a special way to Christ's incarnation, and the cup in a special way to the paschal mystery; or, to put it another way, seeing in the first a mystery of life, and in the second a mystery of love.

A Mystery of Life

The host is the bread of life. Receiving Christ's flesh we receive his life. That life is the nourishment of our lives, not just new strength to restore the wear and tear of living, but the new energy and power that come from the life of God himself. Closely linked to this is the notion of our life with other people. As well as uniting us with Christ, the host unites us with all our brothers and sisters, because we are all one body in Christ. St. Paul in particular underlines this aspect of the bread of life (1 Cor 10:16-17). Holy Communion is not only communion with Christ but communion with one another in him. In saying Amen to the body of Christ, says St Augustine, we say Amen to what we are.

A Mystery of Love

Then there is the Eucharistic cup. Pope John XXIII once said a remarkable thing: 'The most sacred and most mysterious part of the Eucharistic liturgy centres around the chalice of Jesus which contains his precious blood.' If we have already taken the Eucharistic host as the sign of Christ's incarnation, then we can go on to regard the Eucharistic cup as the 'inner sanctum' of the whole celebration. In it we can see especially the most eloquent sign of Christ's death and resurrection by which he draws us into the sacramental mystery in a personal act of sharing with us.

In the cup there are two aspects, form and content. The outward form is a festive cup, reminding us of the resurrection.

If Christ had not risen we would not be celebrating at all, so that the resurrection is the necessary context for any gathering for the Eucharist. It is also, of course, an anticipation of the general resurrection at the end of time, when we are all to come to the goal of it all in the banquet of the kingdom. The inner content of the chalice, however, is nothing less than the blood of Christ. This brings us back to the reality of our lives here below, imparting to us in the struggles of everyday the consolation of his companionship. We can enter into the glory of the resurrection only along the road to Calvary.

Gift of His Heart

But there is more. The ancient writers liked to relate the Eucharistic cup to that mysterious event with which the story of the passion concludes in the Fourth Gospel: one of the soldiers opened his side and immediately there came out blood and water (Jn 19:34). This event, as John implies, was a great sign, and part of what it was revealing was that the ultimate meaning of Calvary, and so of the Eucharist, is to be traced back to the love in the heart of Christ. The blood that flowed from his side and is contained in the chalice is the gift of Christ's heart to each of us. Calvary and the Eucharist are the masterpiece of his love: that is the inmost secret of the mystery of the cup. St Ignatius of Antioch summed it up when he said: 'For drink I desire his blood which is love imperishable.'

Other Lines of Approach

But there are other ways of appreciating the difference between host and cup. Some people relate the host especially to Christ, while the cup puts them in mind of the Holy Spirit. The gift of the Spirit is one of the marks of the new covenant, and the Spirit's presence within us is certainly deepened by the Eucharist. Another way is suggested by the actual words of consecration: it relates the death of Christ to the host and to the strength it gives us for bearing the crosses of life, while thoughts of joy and of the resurrection can go appropriately with the festive cup. Whatever way one prefers, one can see that there is a richness and distinctiveness in each of the Eucharistic gifts. Perhaps the main thing for us is to receive each one as a different gift with a different accent of grace, using whichever of the contrasting lines of approach mentioned above seems most helpful to the individual.

Body and Blood
There is one puzzling feature of this practice which arises out of the words of distribution. We know that every consecrated host contains Christ *as he is now* in heaven, body, blood, soul and divinity. Similarly every Eucharistic cup contains the whole risen Christ, body, blood, soul and divinity. Yet when the host is distributed, the minister says, 'The body of Christ.' When the cup is distributed, the phrase is, 'The blood of Christ.' Nevertheless it would be quite wrong to think that in the host we have only the body of Christ, or that in the chalice we have only the blood of Christ.

The explanation of this strange use of language brings us back to a point made more than once in this book. In the Eucharist, banquet and sacrifice belong together. Holy communion is not only participation in a banquet; it is also participation in a sacrifice. It is a way of showing our fuller commitment to Christ in his sacrifice and so of deepening our union with him in his self-oblation.

The gateway to the resurrection is the cross, and so it is fitting that when the risen Christ comes to us, whole and entire, either through the host or through the cup, he should do so through the memory of that death, which alone made the resurrection possible. As a result, by means of the very act of distribution, the fact of Christ's death is recalled. The whole Christ is present in the host, but under the sign of his body; the whole Christ is present in the cup, but under the sign of his blood. The separate signs remind us of the original separation of his body and blood in death; but that separation has now been overcome by the re-uniting of body, blood, soul and divinity in the glory of his risen state, and that is the total reality in which he is now present to us either in the host or in the cup.

> *The sign of holy communion has a fuller form when administered under both species, since in that way the sign is a clearer expression of the Eucharistic banquet.*
> General Instruction on the Roman Missal

40   THANKSGIVING

'Eucharist' is the Greek word for thanksgiving. The fact that the principal rite of the Christian religion should have such a name suggests that thanksgiving is much more fundamental to our lives than we are normally inclined to think. We will not fully appreciate this name until we see that thanksgiving is as crucial for our lives generally as the sacrament is for our life of faith.

Thanksgiving for Creation
Thanksgiving is a very human thing. It is a measure of our dependence on so much outside ourselves for our day-to-day existence. William Barclay, the Scottish writer on the Bible, expressed that dependence as follows, 'We are all in debt to life. We came into it at the peril of someone's else's life, and we would never have survived without the care of those who loved us.' Gratitude to one's parents is one of the most basic and universal of all human instincts, and few can doubt that to fail in this respect is sub-human if not anti-human. As a line of King

Lear has it, 'How sharper than a serpent's tooth it is to have a thankless child!'

Our debt of gratitude to our parents is the best model we have for our debt of gratitude to God. Great as is our indebtedness to our parents, it is as nothing compared to our indebtedness to God. All day long we come from his hand, and all the good things in our lives are his gifts to us (cf Jas 1:16-17). There is nothing too small or incidental in our lives but that it can be seen as coming to us from his hand (cfr Mt 10:29-31).

The Sunday Obligation

Indeed in this we can see a natural and human basis for our obligation to go to Mass on Sundays. To explain this aspect of our faith we should go deeper than any legal obligation based on canon law or tradition. Our custom in this matter comes ultimately, not just as an obligation of the law, but from an obligation written into human nature itself, once you see your indebtedness to the goodness of God. The Church's tradition of Sunday Mass is simply an authoritative guide as to how this debt may be reasonably honoured. To neglect this obligation is nothing to be proud of! It is just as much a failure in common humanity as is ingratitude to one's parents.

Thanksgiving for Redemption

What we have said so far comes out of the general truth about creation and of our need to worship the Creator; but our obligation to thanksgiving is seen as even more radical when we come to consider Christian revelation. In that teaching God's love for us does not arise because of any goodness in us, but simply because God is love itself. The greatest proof of his love is the fact that Christ loved us when we were still sinners and enemies of God (Rom 5:8; Eph 2:4f). Whatever goodness there might be in us now is not the cause of God's love but its fruit. The failure to acknowledge that fact was the basic flaw in the false thanksgiving of the Pharisee in the parable in Lk 18:11.

There is nothing that we have or are before God which we have not received from his love, and this is the fundamental reason why all our activity before him reduces ultimately to thanksgiving. One of the basic signs of being a Christian redeemed by God's love has to be a heart overflowing with thanksgiving and praise (cfr Col 2:7). This truth was already perceived by the Jews. 'The day will come,' says the Talmud, 'when all prayer will be silent on the lips of people save the prayer of thanksgiving and praise.'

Thanksgiving after Auschwitz

But there is even more to be said. For many people a problem arises when they consider the sin and suffering of the world. One writer put it in an extreme form: *after Auschwitz* can the praise of God be possible on the earth? Our Lord gave us an answer to that difficulty, not so much by what he said as by what he did on the cross.

Greater than the scandal done to any individual in Auschwitz was that done to Christ on Calvary. On one level this event was the greatest act of sacrilege in human history as human beings tortured to death the sinless Son of God. But Christ was greater than anything those men could do to him. In his heart there was the freedom, both human and divine, by which he accepted his Father's will and so transformed his death into a sacrifice. Through the actions of his executioners Calvary was the ultimate in brutality and injustice, but through the action of Christ it became the ultimate in that holiness and love by which the world is saved. Great as is the reality of sin, the reality of grace coming from Christ is greater still (cfr Rom 5:20).

Indeed when we look more closely at the mind and heart of Christ on the cross, though we find there great darkness and anguish, there is still light at the end of the tunnel. Our Lord prayed Psalm 21(22) on the cross. The opening verse is certainly a cry of great desolation (Mk 15:34), but the rest of the psalm reveals how Christ remained united to his Father throughout and had before his mind even the prayer of thanksgiving and praise, Ps 21(22):22ff. The deepest roots of thanksgiving in the Mass lie in that prayer of Christ on the cross. To be able to accept God's will, come what may, and so to praise and thank him, is the ultimate in a Eucharistic attitude to life.

Thanksgiving in Heaven

But the sufferings of Calvary are no more. Christ has overcome, and his prayer of thanksgiving on the cross has reaped a great harvest in the triumphant thanksgiving which he now celebrates in the great liturgy of heaven. One of the greatest truths of the Eucharist, which gives fullness to all the thanksgiving and praise running through the Mass, is the way our sacrifice of praise here on earth rises up into union with that being offered in heaven by Our Lord, by the angels and the saints. This great truth has its main expression in the Eucharistic Prayer, especially at its beginning and at its end. The Preface of every Mass is a hymn to this truth which deserves to be sung more often than is the case. United with the angels and the saints, the Church inevitably wants to burst into song with them around the throne of glory. Holy, Holy, Holy is the Lord. That is the song of the assembly in heaven (Apoc 4:8), and that is the song which we too offer to the Father through, with and in the divine Victim of the Mass.

> *Considered in comparison with the divine bounty, ingratitude is, of all evils imaginable, one of the things most abominable in the eyes of our Creator and Lord.*
> St Ignatius Loyola

41   THE GRACE TO BE GRATEFUL

In this chapter we continue to reflect on the riches contained in the name of this sacrament. The first reason for calling it Eucharist ('thanksgiving') was largely historical, in so far as the sacrament was formed by our Lord and the first Christians out of a Jewish ritual of thanksgiving at table, described earlier in this book. However, in this chapter and in this section of the book, we wish to dig more deeply than history. Here we wish to ask questions about the inner spirit and the view of life which flow from the sacrament; and when we do that, the name of our ritual begins to speak to us in a new way.

A Fundamental Attitude

Thanksgiving is not just another one of those things which it is good for Christians to do. It is the outward expression of a fundamental attitude in life which we might call 'gratefulness'. According to St Paul, a heart overflowing with gratitude is one of the marks of life in grace (Col 2:7). In having our principal Christian sacrament named from this gratefulness and thanksgiving, the Holy Spirit was surely suggesting to us that here we have a fundamental attitude in the living of the Christian life. To appreciate the Eucharist in the first place we must be a grateful people; and a greater gratefulness to God and to those around us is one of the special fruits of this sacrament.

Gratefulness is fundamental for a Christian because it is our response to one of the most fundamental things we can say about our world and our life. The whole world is gift, God's gift to us. Each and every thing in the world, and the whole universe itself, are God's gifts to us, signs of the love with which our Maker has surrounded us. Though we might know this on one level, most of the time we never think of it; but occasionally something happens, and it comes home to us. Maybe we see a glorious sunset; or perhaps it comes through the birth of a baby in the family; or maybe it is just a rose in the garden or a kingfisher on the river-bank. 'Earth's crammed with heaven,' said the poet, 'and every common bush afire with God' (Elizabeth Barrett Browning).

When put like that, thanksgiving, and the gratefulness from which it comes, seem the most natural things in the world and part of the joy of life. But that is not always the way it strikes our twisted human nature. To accept a gift is a way of accepting dependence, and that is not something that pleases our modern world. Maybe we can put it this way,

Two Kinds of People

We can think of two kinds of people and of the difference between them. Modern affluence means that there are many people in our world whose hearts are set on possessions. The love of money is the root of all evil, said the apostle (1 Tim 6:10). When we have too much money we easily tend to become too independent and self-sufficient. These are not necessarily bad things at first, but they can easily lead to pride and a determination not to depend on anyone, even God. So many people today want to be masters of their own lives, make up their own moral law and bow the knee to no one. They are not likely to go to Mass.

The opposite kind of person may or may not be well off, but if they are well off, it has not gone to their heads. They realize that all comes from God, that all is gift, and of ourselves we are nothing. They are happy to see that they are dependent in all kinds of ways: dependent on their families, on their country and on their God. In this way they are happy to be grateful, to acknowledge their dependence, and in their dependence to discover the deeper message, namely that God loves them and surrounds them with his gifts. Out of this gratefulness comes a new and joyous view of life. They will be happy to say 'Thank-you' to God. If they are Catholics, they will normally be happy to say it solemnly and publicly by going to Mass on Sundays. But as well as that, there will be a sense of joy and peace arising from the Mass and remaining with them every day, building up their inward trust in the ever-gracious goodness of God 'from whom all good things come.' Thankfulness is the beginning of a Eucharistic way of life.

Gratefulness and Presence

There are two key aspects of this sacrament which belong together, gratefulness and presence. The more grateful we are to God for everything in our world, the more likely we are to recognize his presence behind everything he has given us. Indeed, not only is he present behind everything that is, but he is present in everything as well. Without his presence in each and everything, that thing simply would not exist. He has to be there to keep it in being.

Sometimes it is easy enough to think of this when we see something beautiful like a flower in the garden or a robin twittering on a branch. But it is true of ordinary things as well. Modern science tells us that each atom is similar to a tiny solar system, with electrons and protons in constant activity, like the planets round the sun. Every atom is a little universe which God maintains in the wonder of its being.

Most of the time we take the world for granted, just as we take God for granted. The once well-known physicist, Arthur Eddington, used to talk of two tables, the table he ate his dinner at and the table he knew as a scientist. The former was brown, solid and made of wood; the other was made of atoms, unimaginable electrons and protons in a vacuum, and it was mostly empty space. Most of the time we are like Eddington at his dinner-table, taking the world for granted; but the world of protons and electrons, with God at its centre, is the world as it really is, God's gift to us for our lives.

The link, then, in the Eucharist between thanksgiving and presence gives us a key for unlocking something of God's view of the world. Though thanksgiving and presence belong together in the Eucharist in an altogether unique way, they are nevertheless mirrored in the world generally, once we see it as God sees it. The more grateful we are to God for all the persons and things that form our world, the more clearly will we see them all as God's gift to us; and the more this view of things comes home to us, the deeper will be our sense of his presence in our lives. Thanksgiving then is the gateway to the mystery of divine presence, in one way at Mass, in another way throughout our lives.

All Is Gift
With thanksgiving and presence at its heart, the Eucharist is really a lesson to us about the kind of world we live in. As in the Eucharist, so in the world, thanksgiving helps the sense of God's presence, and that very sense of presence increases our debt of gratitude. On the one hand we thank God because he is present, in one way in the Eucharist and in another way in the world. On the other hand, the more open we are to gratefulness and thanksgiving, the more sensitive we become to the truth that all is gift, and so the more conscious we become of the Giver behind everything that is.

Ignatius Loyola used to speak of 'finding God in all things,' but he was also convinced that the key to such a view of the world lies in gratitude. One of his contemporaries wrote of him: 'From seeing a plant, foliage, a leaf, a flower, any fruit, from the consideration of a little worm or any other animal, he raised himself above the heavens and penetrated the deepest thoughts.' With this view of things in one's heart, one is ready for the truth that the wonder of the divine presence overflows the Eucharist and is something which can be sought at every time and place. Every moment of our lives can be a kind of 'sacrament' and so an opportunity for thanksgiving and praise.

> *I shall ask for an inner knowledge of so many and such great benefits received from God so that, fully conscious of my indebtedness, I may in all things love and serve the Divine Majesty.*
>
> St Ignatius Loyola

42   TRANSFORMING THE WORLD

As Our Lord said farewell to the disciples before his ascension, in the scene recounted in Mt 28:16-20, he opened up before their eyes the prospect of a mission without limit on which he was launching them. 'Go therefore and teach all nations...' In a way that they could not yet have realized, he was sending them out to change the world. This was the fire he had come to cast upon the earth (Lk 12:49).

A Prophet's Vision

At that point of time such a project scarcely seemed practical. Two thousand years later we can see that Christianity has changed much of the world, but even yet it has still a long way to go. In fact Our Lord's dream is not to be judged simply in the terms of an historian. It belongs rather to the vision of a prophet looking to the ultimate transformation of all things by God at the end of time. As we saw in an earlier chapter, Christian revelation looks forward to a great final event of consummation, when there will be a new heaven and a new earth (2 Pet 3:12-13), and God will be all in all (1 Cor 15:28).

This visionary element in Our Lord's teaching betrays a divine discontent with the world as it is. It is not just the world of the apostles' day which had to be changed. The world of our times also falls short of the divine plan, but the visionary force

of Christ remains to inspire us all and to remind us how he has
never relinquished his mission to change the minds and hearts
of the human race.

The Place of the Eucharist

In this mission the Eucharist of Christ has a central role. The very
institution of the sacrament as an ongoing sign of the work of
redemption, reveals Our Lord's desire to let the Eucharist change
us, so that we in turn might help in changing the world. The
Eucharist is all about change: Christ in the Eucharist changing
bread and wine; the transformed bread and wine helping to
change us; we in turn helping to change the world.

There are many Christians who do not see the Eucharist
that way, because they do not see Christianity that way. Many
of them can think of this world only as a place of sin, and they
see themselves as the holy remnant, the elect of God, in the
world but not of it, simply awaiting their Master's return,
which sometimes they understand as anticipated in the
Eucharist. For others the Eucharist is entirely about the next
life. It is our window on another world, or a kind of filling-
station, which just helps us to keep going on our journey to
heaven. For people like this the Eucharist is not really saying
anything about this world nor about the kingdom which is
being brought to birth within it.

The New Earth Has Begun

We Catholics see things somewhat differently. Though there is
evil in the world, there is also good. Indeed something of the
glory of the future has already entered the present, and the
proof of this can be found in the resurrection of Christ. At that
point Christ's human nature, body and soul, was given the gifts
and qualities of a glorified existence. The way Our Lord's risen
body entered through closed doors (Jn 20:19) was a sign of a

more fundamental change. Already in his flesh 'the new earth' was beginning.

Similarly in the Eucharist, where the same glorified flesh is given to us, we meet another manifestation of the 'new earth.' Truly the risen Christ is at work in the Eucharist to touch our lives with the energy and power of another world, but this 'other world' is not totally other! It is the world into which this one is being changed, as the transforming power of Christ's love reaches into human hearts.

Transforming Life

From all this it follows that the Eucharistic way of faith is called to be a force for change in the world. If we are devoted to the Eucharist, we cannot be content with the world in which we live. It is too easy just to sit back and accept the limitations of our present situation. The idealism of young people in particular, their desire to better their fellow human beings, can find in the Eucharist inspiration and strength. All of us, young and old, having due regard for age and circumstances, will discover in the sacrament a power that helps transform life and gives it a meaning and a depth which we otherwise could not attain.

In particular we might relate what we have said to devotion to the tabernacle. Because of the atmosphere of quiet and contemplation which surrounds the tabernacle, it is easy for this devotion to become a kind of escape from reality; but this is hardly being true to the body that was offered for the sake of others. It will help if we see Our Lord's presence in the tabernacle as part of his transforming mission. He is here presenting us with part of that new heaven and new earth already anticipated in his flesh. Our Lord is in the tabernacle transforming the world, transforming us so that we might help to transform others.

From the perpetuation of the sacrifice of the cross and her communion with the body and blood of Christ in the Eucharist, the Church draws the spiritual power needed to carry out her mission.

John Paul II

43   SIGN OF GRACE

In an earlier chapter in this book it was noted that the sense of the presence of God in our lives gradually becomes second-nature to those who are regular participants in the Eucharist and devoted to the Blessed Sacrament. The sacramental signs have their own way of working upon us and of speaking to our minds and hearts, but in this present chapter we will try to spell out in explicit terms how this particular message is conveyed in the sacrament.

God Living Within Us

All the wonderful teaching in the New Testament about God and Christ and their work among us eventually comes to centre on the extraordinary truth of the divine indwelling. The three persons of the Trinity really live within those who are friends of God. Of the Holy Spirit, Our Lord says, 'He will be continually at your side, nay, he will be in you' (Jn 14:17); and of the Father and Son he says, 'If any love me, my Father will love them, and we will come to them and make our home in them' (Jn 14:23). This truth about God living within us is the centre-piece of the Catholic doctrine of grace. You might ask, What is grace? Well grace is life; it is nothing less than the divine life shared with us, in which Father, Son and Holy Spirit give themselves to us and remain with us.

Now the Eucharist itself is one of the main signs to us of this truth about the nature of divine grace, but to appreciate this we might have to broaden our notion of what goes to make up the Eucharistic sign. In this sacrament the sign is not just the bread and the wine changed into Christ's body and blood. These are but part of the sign. The sign also lies in the event of distribution where the minister, representing Christ himself, gives us the body and blood of the Lord. The minister, male or female, clerical or lay, is part of the sign. What is immediately signified is Christ giving us himself; the sign is the minister giving us the sacrament.

The Eucharist as Sign of Grace

But in addition to this immediate meaning, there is a longer-term meaning as well. Christ giving us himself in the sacrament is really a sign to us of what grace is. The sacramental self-gift is a sign of the divinity giving itself to us and remaining within us in the mystery of divine grace. The sacrament is the clearest indication to us of what it means that in the mystery of grace God gives us himself. The sacramental self-gift by Christ is over in a moment, and the Eucharistic presence of Christ's body and blood does not last very long, but these events take place only in view of the other longer-term gift of the divine indwelling. They are at once its sign and its cause. The self-gift of Christ in the sacrament is fulfilled when it brings about a deepening within us of God's continuing self-gift to the soul in the state of grace.

But there is yet more to be said. A second aspect of the sacrament helps to confirm and deepen the message already conveyed in the mystery of holy communion. I refer to the presence of Christ in the tabernacle. This mystery of continuing presence teaches us something about the way divine presence, once given, is not withdrawn unless extinguished by our actions. The permanence of the presence in the tabernacle points to the permanence of the presence in grace. The first is part of the sign, while the second belongs to that which is signified. From the one we become more aware of the other, and the one helps to nourish and deepen the reality of the other.

God With Us

When the second person of the Trinity descended from heaven to be born as a little baby, he was coming among us to remain with us for ever. From that time on he would always be 'Emmanuel', that is 'God with us' (Mt 1:23). Even when he went back to heaven on the day of his Ascension, he was not really withdrawing his presence from us, but only the visibility of his presence. This reveals to us that once Christ comes, he wishes to remain with those to whom he comes. The same truth is revealed in the Eucharist. Around every tabernacle we can write 'Emmanuel', the God who wishes to remain with us. Every time he comes to us in holy communion this same desire of his is at work, namely to remain with us always through the mystery of divine grace.

The Eucharist as Centre of the World of Faith

Clearly these are extraordinary mysteries of God's desire to be involved in our lives, yet not only are they central to our faith in the Eucharist, they are central to the life of faith as such. The mystery of divine indwelling is the centre-piece of revelation and faith. Indeed the life of faith can be summed up as our conscious response to this truth about God's presence within us. When we see how the Eucharist is a privileged instance of the truth about grace, we get another insight into the central role of the Eucharist for the entire life of faith and prayer.

Unfortunately a life of more intense prayer and deeper faith can often seem to be the pursuit of only an elite. On the other hand these riches of Eucharistic truth are available to all who come to the Lord's table. Furthermore, as was said above, the sacrament has its own language and its own mode of communication, and there is consolation in the fact that it often conveys its message to people who could not put it into words. Nevertheless it is helpful when the truth is spelt out in clear terms, and it is surely desirable that more and more of the ordinary faithful be given a clearer idea of these unsearchable riches of Christ which are their birth-right and their heritage as sons and daughters of God and guests at his table.

O sacred banquet in which Christ is consumed, the memory of his passion is recalled, the mind is filled with grace and there is given to us a pledge of a future life without end.
Medieval Antiphon